Humorous, Serious, and Thoughtful Ideas

Israel Drazin

Humorous, Serious, and Thoughtful Ideas

Copyright ©Israel Drazin
Jerusalem 2024
תשפ"ד/5784

All rights reserved. No part of this publication may be translated, reproduced, stored in a retrieval system, or transmitted, in any form or by any means, electronic, mechanical, photocopying, recording or otherwise, without express written permission from the publishers.

Cover Design: Leah Ben Avraham/Noonim Graphics
Typesetting: www.optumetech.com

ISBN: 978-965-7801-74-1

Gefen Books
c/o Baker & Taylor Publisher Services
30 Amberwood Parkway
Ashland, Ohio 44805
516-593-1234
orders@gefenpublishing.com

Gefen Publishing House Ltd.
6 Hatzvi Street
Jerusalem 9438614,
Israel
972-2-538-0247
orders@gefenpublishing.com

www.gefenpublishing.com

Printed in Israel

Library of Congress Control Number: 2024945122

Dedicated as usual with love to my wife Dina, my inspiration
who makes it possible for me to write books and articles

Fifty-two books by Israel Drazin

Maimonides and Rational Series
Maimonides: Reason Above All
Maimonides and the Biblical Prophets
Maimonides: The Extraordinary Mind
A Rational Approach to Judaism and Torah Commentary
Nachmanides: An Unusual Thinker
What We Don't Know about God and People in the Hebrew Bible: Genesis
What We Don't Know about God and People in the Hebrew Bible: Exodus
What We Don't Know about God and the People in the Bible: Leviticus
What We Don't Know about God and the People in the Bible: Numbers

Mysteries of Judaism
Mysteries of Judaism I
Mysteries of Judaism II: How the Rabbis and Others Changed Judaism
Mysteries of Judaism III: Common Sense Evaluations of Religious Thoughts
Mysteries of Judaism IV: Over 100 Mistaken Ideas about God and the Bible
Mysteries of Judaism V: More than 150 Mistaken Ideas about God and the Bible
Stories that Teach the Truth

Unusual Bible Interpretation series
Five Books of Moses
Joshua
Judges
Ruth, Esther, and Judith
Jonah and Amos
Hosea

Other Books on the Bible
Who Was the Biblical Samuel?
The Tragedies of King David
Who Really Was the Biblical David?
The Authentic King Solomon
Who Really Was the Biblical Elijah?

Scholarly Targum Books:
Targumic Studies
Targum Onkelos to Exodus
Targum Onkelos to Leviticus
Targum Onkelos to Numbers
Targum Onkelos to Deuteronomy

Novel
She Wanted to Be Jewish

Editor of and forewords to Nathan Drazin's books:
Legends Worth Living
Abraham - The Father of the Jewish People

With Cecil B. Currey:
For God and Country

With Stanley Wagner:
Understanding the Bible Text: Onkelos on the Torah: Genesis
Understanding the Bible Text: Onkelos on the Torah: Exodus
Understanding the Bible Text: Onkelos on the Torah: Leviticus
Understanding the Bible Text: Onkelos on the Torah: Numbers
Understanding the Bible Text: Onkelos on the Torah: Deuteronomy
Understanding Onkelos
Beyond the Bible Text
Iyunim Betargum (Hebrew)

With Leba Lieder
Can't Start Passover without the Bread
Sailing on Moti's Ark on Succoth
Just What the Doctor Ordered: Moti's Purim Story

As Daniel A. Diamond

Around the World in 123 Days

Chaos on the Victoria: Around the World in 78 Days, Almost

Rational Religion

Eleven forewords to books by Rabbi Dr. Michael Leo Samuel

Maimonides' Hidden Torah Commentary, Genesis, Book One

Maimonides' Hidden Torah Commentary, Genesis, Book Two

Maimonides' Hidden Torah Commentary, Exodus, Book One

Maimonides' Hidden Torah Commentary, Exodus, Book Two

Maimonides' Hidden Torah Commentary, Leviticus

Maimonides' Hidden Torah Commentary, Numbers

Maimonides' Hidden Torah commentary, Deuteronomy

An Odyssey of Faith

Gentle Jewish wisdom

Birth and Rebirth Through Genesis 1–11

Birth and Rebirth Through Genesis 12–27

Acknowledgments

I want to thank Darlene Jospe, who edited the first version of this book, as she did virtually all my books for many decades, and Ruth Pepperman, who did the final checking and proofreading of this book.

Contents

Introduction	xv
Chapter One – Intelligence and Humor	1
Chapter Two – Are We Descendants of King David?	3
Chapter Three – It Isn't Easy to Work Out the Descent from David	5
Chapter Four – Applying the Population Statistics to Spain	7
Chapter Five – Applying the Population Statistics to Hitler	9
Chapter Six – What Assures Success	11
Chapter Seven – Weather Forecasting	13
Chapter Eight – The Current Calendar	15
Chapter Nine – The Truth about the Untrue "Since Creation Calendar"	17
Chapter Ten – Three and Seven	21
Chapter Eleven – The Commercial Company Staff Meeting	23
Chapter Twelve – Plagiarism International	27
Chapter Thirteen – Reincarnation	29
Chapter Fourteen – Is Reincarnation a Fact, a Lie, or a Truth?	31
Chapter Fifteen – Beliefs	35
Chapter Sixteen – My List of Three Basic Principles of Judaism	37
Chapter Seventeen – Two Torah Messages Often Missed	41
Chapter Eighteen – The Truth about Facts and Jokes	45
Chapter Nineteen – The Truth Is the Truth, No Matter What Its Source	47
Chapter Twenty – Crowd Jokes	49
Chapter Twenty-One – The Crowd Instinct and Power	51
Chapter Twenty-Two – Meat-Eater Jokes	53
Chapter Twenty-Three – Michael's Trip to Heaven	55
Chapter Twenty-four – A Possible Solution to Why There Is Evil	59

xiv · HUMOROUS, SERIOUS, AND THOUGHTFUL IDEAS

Chapter Twenty-Five – The History of Shoes and Clothing 63

Chapter Twenty-Six – Ethical Behaviors Concerning Shoes 65

Chapter Twenty-Seven – Rashi: Marvelous but Irrational 69

Chapter Twenty-Eight – Unknown Facts about the Bible 79

Chapter Twenty-Nine – To Whom Do We Pray? 85

Chapter Thirty – What Do We Know about God? 95

Chapter Thirty-One – Two Surprising Changes by Jews 97

Sources 99

Index 101

Brigadier General Israel Drazin 105

Introduction

People should strive to learn how to improve themselves and act intelligently. Maimonides said that God does not directly help people but that He gave them intelligence in order to help them make decisions in life. It is their God-given intelligence that can help them. Maimonides also said that we can learn from everything God created, to which I agree.

We can learn from our own body. As we will see later in this book, Elias Canetti taught that even the human body teaches lessons. Humans learned from the nails on their index fingers how to make knives, spears, and arrows. From their thumbs he maintained that they learned to make bows for the arrows. The earlier rabbis taught that we can learn much from animals, even ethics from ants. Maimonides said. "The truth is the truth no matter what its source."

I am convinced that we can learn from all writings, even jokes, a few of which I have I included in this book. If people took a little time after hearing a joke to wonder why we laugh, what it is about a particular joke that provokes laughter, what we can learn from it, and how its lesson may apply at other times, I firmly believe that in this way we can bring about improvement in ourselves and society.

Sometimes, after these jokes I suggest thoughts to ponder, which hopefully might encourage the reader to think of an idea.

In addition to jokes, I included other essays to make us think and improve ourselves, some serious, and others humorous. I have several chapters in which I address the subject of statistics in a somewhat humorous fashion. All science is based on statistics. Our lives are based on statistics. However, statistics only tell us the possibility of the truth, not the certainty of it. What should we learn from this?

WHAT CAUSES US TO LAUGH?

Frequently, laughing shows our joy or happiness in overcoming embarrassment, confusion, or an obvious conclusion. Why would a joke such as, "Why did the chicken cross the street? To get to the other side" trigger us to laugh? Is it because we did not know the answer before it was given and were surprised in its simplicity?

WHAT DOES THAT TEACH US?

Laughter is also considered an evolutionary mechanism that helps build social bonds and regulate human relationships. What does that teach us that we can apply to other occasions?

A laugh or a smile can make you feel better in difficult times. I found that in the rare times that I am sad, if I force myself to smile, my body may respond in kind to the point that I have a brighter outlook.

Chapter One
Intelligence and Humor

It seems to me that an intelligent person has to have a sense of humor.

I then wondered if God, with the highest intelligence, might have a highly developed sense of humor. Of course, once I realized that I had just opened a Pandora's box, I stopped thinking about this further.

POINTS TO PONDER

People who believe no proof is necessary, go through life accepting nonsense.

Some people see a dot as a sign to stop. Others see it as a prompt to think, an opportunity to expand one's imagination and knowledge.

People are convinced that beliefs better their lives, but fail to see that their beliefs keep them chained within them. They need to think, not blindly accept.

Chapter Two
Are We Descendants of King David?

Statistically speaking, it is possible.

David could have had millions of descendants, and we might be among them.

David lived about three thousand years ago. Scholars generally consider a generation as twenty or thirty years. This means over ninety generations have existed since David's children were born. David had more than two children. But since there were many early deaths, forced conversions, and killings during these years, let's be conservative and assign a birth of two children for each of the ninety generations.

If we start the count with 2 children being born, in the second generation, the 2 children will have 4 children. In the third, the 4 will have 8. The fourth, 16. The fifth, 32. The sixth generation, 64, the seventh, 128. The eighth, 256. The ninth, 512. The tenth, 1,024. The eleventh, 2,048.

If we simplify the count by rounding it down from 2,048 to 2,000, in the twelfth of the ninety generations, there would be 4,000. The thirteenth, 8,000. The fourteenth, 16,000. The fifteenth 32,000. Then, 64,000, 128,000, 256,000, 512,000, and then over a million with over sixty generations to go.

The numbers increase enormously from then on. By the end of the ninety generations, the total would be massive. There are so many descendants that it seems possible that every Jew alive today would be a descendant of David.

HOWEVER, THERE IS A PROBLEM.
There is a famous quote, "Lies, damned lies, and statistics." It is a phrase describing the persuasive power of statistics to bolster weak arguments.

4 · HUMOROUS, SERIOUS, AND THOUGHTFUL IDEAS

On the other hand, most, if not all of the sciences involve statistics. What does this tell us about science?

Do statistics not show that every Jew alive today, as well as every non-Jew, may be a descendant of King David?

Do we believe what this statistic tells us?

Chapter Three
It Isn't Easy to Work Out the Descent from David

In the two New Testament Gospels, Matthew has twenty-seven generations from King David to Joseph, the husband of Mary, whereas Luke has forty-two. There is virtually no overlap between the two, or with other alleged genealogies.

POINTS TO PONDER
Why do we think it is significant that we had a famous ancestor?

How should we accept biblical, ancestral listings?

Why did the ancients believe ancestors came back as ghosts to haunt us?

Did the ancients place stones over graves to hold their dead underground and make it difficult for them to rise?

Chapter Four
Applying the Population Statistics to Spain

In 1478, King Ferdinand II of Aragon and Queen Isabella I of Castile, Spain, established the Holy Office of the Inquisition, commonly known as the Spanish Inquisition, to combat heresy and forcibly convert Jews to Roman Catholicism. Many Jews were converted.

History and statistics tell us that these converted Jews intermarried with non-Jewish Spaniards over the ensuing 545 years, over eighteen generations. If we call Jewish ancestry "Jewish Blood," isn't it possible that most, if not all, Spaniards today have Jewish blood?

POINTS TO PONDER

Does this mean that the Inquisition failed in its mission?

Isn't this an example of how zealousness in religion leads to the opposite of what religion is meant to teach?

Aren't there hundreds of examples of this? For instance, the Crusades, and the desire to conquer other countries, including the Spanish, French, and English conquest of America and Canada from the native inhabitants, the misguided treatment of Indians in India, and Jews in pre-Israel Palestine by the British who claimed they were only trying to help those people.

Chapter Five
Applying the Population Statistics to Hitler

When we recognize that the statistics in chapter two apply to a single man among the close to a million, more or less, Jews who lived at the time of King David, we realize that by applying the statistics to the many Jews, there is the possibility that many people alive today have Jewish blood. This would include Adolph Hitler.

The 2010 British *Daily Telegraph* reported a study of saliva taken from thirty-nine Hitler relatives whose DNA was tested. The study revealed a rare chromosome in Western Europe, but frequent among Jews. However, scientists say that while the study is scientific, it is inconclusive.

POINTS TO PONDER

Should we compare this idea to that of the rabbis who said that the Torah describes all humanity as descendants of a single couple, Adam and Eve, to emphasize that we are all equal and should be treated as such?

Why do we think Hitler was evil?

Chapter Six
What Assures Success

Too many people claim they cannot achieve any success because of problems they had in the past.

Let us use the example of a particular man who had to leave school at age ten to help support his family.

As a child, he was emotionally and physically abused by his drunken father and whipped for any supposed mistake.

He was once mistakenly arrested as a tramp, and began losing his hearing at age twenty-eight, becoming deaf at the age of forty-four.

Although in love twice, he could not marry his love because he was a commoner and had a low economic status. Thus, he never married and had no children.

Even with this man's difficult past, he became one of the most significant, respected, admired, and influential classical music composers.

His name was Ludwig van Beethoven.

POINTS TO PONDER
Successful people may be so because they worked hard, and not due to their IQ.

Success is related to action.

Nothing is altogether impossible.

As simple as the statement "If life serves you lemons, make lemonade" is, it is sound advice.

Chapter Seven
Weather Forecasting

Using the predictions of the internet, which in its variance is perchance "almost" always right:

"A seven-day forecast can accurately predict the weather about 80 percent of the time, and a five-day forecast can accurately predict the weather approximately 90 percent. However, a ten-day or longer forecast that is given frequently is only right about half the time."

When weather forecasters always put on a smile and tell us, along with a joke to distract us, what the forecast is, one can place a smile on his/her face, tell a joke, toss a coin, and be right as often as the forecaster. Or one can just look out the window and make a more precise, up-to-date prediction, which most likely is correct 60 percent of the time.

The funniest superstition is that if the forecast calls for rain, and one takes an umbrella, it will not rain, but if one leaves the umbrella behind it will rain for sure.

POINTS TO PONDER

How many times have we accepted what we are told and do not, metaphorically speaking, look out the window?

What is the difference between weather forecasters and biblical false prophets?

Chapter Eight
The Current Calendar

I am writing this on "New Year's Day," January 1, 2024.

The calculation that led to this year being 2024 is the Christian version. It was invented in 525 AD, which was used in the past and means "The Year of the Lord" (Jesus) in English. BC was used to indicate "Before Christ." Today, most scholars use CE for "Common Era" and BCE for "Before the Common Era."

The author of this calendar presumed that he was calculating based on the birth of Jesus. He believed that Jesus was born in the year 1, but this is a mistake. A careful reading of the New Testament shows that Jesus was born sometime between 6 and 4 BCE.

The author forgot that in the New Testament Gospel, Matthew 2:16, Joseph and Mary were visited by an angel who told them Herod would attempt to kill Jesus, their son. Herod died in 4 BCE. So, Jesus was born four to six years BCE.

POINTS TO PONDER

While this is a significant mistake, it is not unusual. Every human makes mistakes.

How can we learn to recognize mistakes from what we are told or taught?

Children are taught ideas meant for education in Sunday schools, but these are not the same ideas understood by adults. Yet, as they grow older, they retain these ideas and not those that are rational and true. How can they learn the truth?

To show that I am not mocking Christianity, see the following chapter.

Chapter Nine
The Truth about the Untrue "Since Creation Calendar"

People from different cultures, secular or religious, with diverse worldviews, have attempted to calculate the age of the world. There is no agreement among them simply because it is an impossible task. Christians, Muslims, and Jews have tried to do the calculation based on a literal reading of the Bible and have come up with different times. The following shows the impossibility by focusing on the widely used Jewish version.[1]

We do not know when some Jews first thought to calculate years from creation. We understand that the talmudic rabbis knew nothing of this calendar, called "anno mundi," meaning "year (of the) world," and thus used the Greek calendar. Scholars, such as Azariah de' Rossi, in his *The Light of the Eyes*, speculate that the anno mundi may have originated around the sixth century, after the Talmudic Period.[2] While this seems to be the date of its origin, it was not until relatively recently that Jews began to use it. Maimonides, for example, dated his documents with the Greek calendar in the thirteenth century. Jews adopted it recently simply because many forgot about its origin and thought it was a divine revelation to the Israelites at Mount Sinai. Other Jews accepted it because it is a "tradition, and one doesn't question traditions."

---

1. When Rosh Hashana, the New Year, started in September 2023, the Jewish anno mundi year was 5784 (since creation). This widely used calendar dates the patriarch Abraham's birth to 1948 anno mundi (c. 1813 BCE), the same year the State of Israel was reestablished according to the currently-used secular calendar. It dates the giving of the Ten Commandments as 2448, which would be 3,336 years before September 2023.
2. The same time the Christian calendar was invented.

18 · HUMOROUS, SERIOUS, AND THOUGHTFUL IDEAS

Jewry had good reasons for initially rejecting this calendar. There are theological, practical, and logical reasons why it is clear that the anno mundi is incorrect. The anno mundi inventor calculated the years since creation by taking biblical numbers literally. He relied on imaginative, non-factual, midrashic speculations of dates when the Bible was unclear. He accepted traditions about periods developed to teach homiletical lessons and not historical facts. Scholars feel that biblical time frames and dating were meant to be taken with a grain of salt. The Bible is not a history book. It is designed to teach about the existence of God and proper behavior.

The world may have been created over a very long period, humans may not have appeared on earth until millions of years had passed, and the average life span before the flood may not have been hundreds of years, as seems to be indicated by a literal reading of the Bible. When the Torah states that Adam lived for 930 years, it may refer to years that lasted from one lunar cycle to the next, about 29.5 days. If the 930 "years" are divided by twelve (months), the result is 77.5 currently-calculated years, the average lifespan today. Even if the world was created in a single day, Adam did not die in the year 930 but in 77.[3]

The anno mundi is based on Midrashim. For example, scripture states that Noah bore three sons when he was 500 years old: Shem, Ham, and Yaphet. A midrash states that they were not all born in the same year.[4] According to the midrash, Shem was not the oldest son and was born when his father was 502. The anno mundi is based on Shem's midrashic birthday, contrary to the biblical text's plain reading.

Another problem with using the anno mundi is that some of the periods listed in the Bible are questionable. For example, it is possible to date the judges in the book of Judges one after the other, as the book implies, and insist, as does the anno mundi, that the period of the judges lasted over five hundred years.[5]

---

3. It is possible that after the flood, the calculation of years changed, and people considered the difference from a warm to a cold season as a year, so two biblical years during this period are equal to one year today. While the Bible states that Abraham lived 175 years, Isaac 180, Joseph 110, and Moses 120, they would have died at ages 87, 90, 55, and 60, respectively.

4. This midrash is not based on anything in the Bible and is contrary to what is stated.

5. I Kings 6:1 seems to say the period lasted 360 years from the entry of the Israelites into Canaan until the onset of King Saul's reign.

However, it is more reasonable to suppose that some judges must have overlapped since they served in different tribes. We cannot determine by how much, and scholars state the period was only about two hundred years.

Similarly, when the Bible says that a king ruled for a certain number of years, it is unclear, even as the Talmud recognizes, whether the first and last years are full years of twelve months or parts of a calendar year. In the latter case, two kings would have ruled in the same year, affecting the anno mundi calculation.

Additionally, most post-biblical events are based on questionable traditions. Tradition states that the Second Temple stood for 420 years, while scholars count the Second Temple period as over 580 years, from 516 BCE to 70 CE. The anno mundi also assigns dates for people not even hinted at in Scripture; for instance, we have yet to learn how long King Saul reigned.

In short, some people take the Bible literally and do not accept the basic assumptions used by the anno mundi calculations. Some people take the Bible literally, but develop different calculations of the periods mentioned because they interpret the events differently. Many do not accept the literal words in the Torah. Nevertheless, some Jews are convinced that it is a religious duty to use this calendar and feel good when they date their correspondence with the anno mundi year.

Chapter Ten

Three and Seven

The numbers three and seven occur frequently in many cultures. Some see the number seven as signifying a complete act, such as creating the world in seven days. It is followed by eight, which signifies a new beginning, as when Jewish boys are circumcised on the eighth day after birth. Others see seven as part of nature as in the seven planets, or in counting seven human parts: two legs, two arms, an upper and lower body part, and a head.

From a somewhat humorous side, seven completes the number of lies: (1) White lies such as, "She sure is a lovely bride." (2) Noble lies, also called Essential Truths, are those in which "God becomes angry when people misbehave." They are told to unsophisticated folks who must believe the falsehoods to control their behavior. (3) Common falsehoods like, "I never said you are a fool." (4) Statistics, "It will rain tomorrow at 6 p.m." (5) Terrible lies when a defendant tells the judge. "Honestly, I didn't kill the bitch." (6) Newspaper, radio, and TV lies, "Evidence shows that.…" Without a proper investigation, only self-serving assurances. (7) Political lies are when politicians tell the community only what helps them collect funds and assure reelection. They hide the truth and tell themselves that the public is better served not knowing.

There are some who think that three is almost half of seven and indicates a minor effort. However, while seven is usually used positively, three often involves something terrible or incomplete. Snow White has seven dwarfs who help her, but in each of the stories of the three bears and three pigs, one of them gets into trouble. The Bible has Abraham taking his son Isaac to be sacrificed and traveling for three days, thinking it was the will of God, yet God did not want a human sacrifice. The same Bible told the Israelites to prepare for the divine revelation for three days. Should it have been seven? After the revelation, the

Israelites sacrificed to a golden calf, not God. Like Shakespeare's three witches in Macbeth making three dire prophecies, witchcraft uses the number three frequently. Many teachers of clerics suggest their disciples keep their ideas down to three to facilitate their congregants' understanding, but a sizable number snooze anyway. Does the number three, which does not quite make it to half of seven, suggest that people should not make halfway endeavors, but persevere and do a complete job?

Chapter Eleven
The Commercial Company Staff Meeting

This is the transcript of the January 2, 2024, "Helpful Commercial Company" Staff Meeting.

Boss: Thanks, staff, for coming in today despite it being a holiday. But what we do for our country is essential. Commercials are fundamental to capitalism, the economy, and a satisfied society. Before we explore new ideas for 2024, you need to know this.

Everyone must attend our protest demonstration in front of the White House next week. We need to get people to realize that the eighteen-minute commercial restriction is barbaric and misinformed and will collapse our democracy. Our lawyers tell us it violates the US Constitution. In the early days of TV, brutal laws prohibited more than one commercial from being inserted in each TV segment. Today, wiser minds allow as many as we like but still limit us to eighteen minutes during each sixty-minute feature. We demand twenty. The time has come for society to recognize the need. That's why we're protesting.

Every man must wear a tie at the protest. Every female must wear a skirt no lower than the knees. True, many businessmen and women have revolted against better dressing. But we are better than our clients, the business people. We at "Helpful Commercial" are the force that makes them successful. We are a father to them. We need to show it by what we wear.

Sammy, I can tell by your inability to sit still that you have an idea for us. What is it?

Sammy: I want to address the problem we discussed often. I did a statistical study. Eighty-four thousand and sixty-two phone calls were made to our clients objecting to the demand we placed in many of our commercials telling them to ask their doctors about our product. Most blasted us, screaming that we've no right to make demands. Two thousand and ninety-two doctors filed suit in courts protesting the demand, arguing that the questions take too much of their time and make them lose money. The AMA joined these suits. True, our demand to call the doctors informed them about our product, which is good. But at what cost? We need to address this problem.

Jim: I have an idea. We all know the current trend to fill our eighteen-minute allotment by allowing our clients to repeat the same commercial back-to-back four times. We also know the public complaints that we are acting as if they're stupid, that they can't get the point the first time. I see a solution. We end the fourth repetition by asking viewers which of the four repetitions is most informative.

Harold: That's stupid! They're all the same.

Jim: Sure they are. But by challenging them with this question, we're forcing them to watch the commercial a fifth and even a sixth time. They won't find a distinction. But we will tire them out, and they'll lose the energy to complain. After six repetitions, they unconsciously want to buy what we are selling. Adolph Hitler taught us that if you repeat a lie enough times, people will believe it.

Boss: Stop that banging on our table showing you agree. OK, the suggestion is accepted. But as I previously warned you, this is the last time doing it. The table is old and fragile. If you guys break it, you'll pay for it.

Marsha: I have an idea of how to add viewers. We include minorities in the commercials, but we forgot that half of our population is overweight. We need to have at least one fat person in each commercial.

Boss: I warned you guys. Stop the table banging!

Marsha: Thanks everyone for your agreement. I have another idea. It's about the current practice to have our commercials contain a drama that has nothing to do with the product. Let's apply it to the cosmetic industry. I'll show you two ways to have the drama and highlight our product. We can place a car on a spaceship to the moon, land it, and drive it to the dark back of the moon over treacherous and adventurous territory. Then the driver steps out of the car into the headlights holding our client's cream and says with pride, "Our … even keeps us warm in the dark, cold areas of the moon!"

Boss: One more time, and I'm sure the table will crumble.

Marsha: Thanks again, fellows. The moon idea is for areas with cold climates. I have one for the overly warm ones. This time, the driver drives over terrible roads to Hell. He enters the region where Adolph Hitler is sitting in a burning barrel. Hitler stretches out his hand. It contains our product. He smiles and says, "Even here, … cools my body!"

Boss: Morton, you are the Aristotle of our company. You always come up with startling ideas. Do you have one today?

Morton: I do. Why demand only twenty minutes? Let's shoot for twenty-five and settle for twenty-two.

Boss: Now you've done it! Each of you will have $17.48 deducted from your next salary to pay for our new table.

Chapter Twelve
Plagiarism International

The following are excerpts from testimonies before the US House Committee on January 22, 2023, by the president of Plagiarism International, Dr. Horatio Arnold, PhD, DD. Dr. Arnold was chosen for this position when it was revealed that he had the distinction of plagiarizing his PhD thesis from five scholars, yet his Doctor of Philosophy advisor overlooked this skill. In addition, since he plagiarized a Muslim dissertation for his Doctor of Divinity, he changed the name from Mohammed to Jesus, and Allah to God.

Dr Arnold informed his audience, "Plagiarism International is a worldwide organization. In the US, it includes two former US presidents, one hundred and twenty members of the US Congress, six college presidents, and one thousand and twenty-five clergy.

"Our motto is, 'Don't let a good idea lie dormant in the dark grave of history when you can resurrect it to life in the present healthy world to be enjoyed by others.'

"Plagiarism is like adoption. A woman may be the natural parent of a child. But the adoptive parent gives the child a new name and a new life. It is often better to not reveal the name of the birth mother to the child.

"The Plagiarism International prayer is: 'Dear Lord, give me the wisdom to recognize good ideas, make them my own, and give them a life with me as their parent.'"

During his inspiring testimony, an excited congressman, Lenard Hill, interrupted another congressman and shouted at Dr. Arnold, "You stole an idea from me!" Dr. Arnold responded, "So I did. God bless us both. For He surely did."

After this discourteous interruption, Dr. Arnold explained, "Plagiarism is not illegal in the US. It is considered a violation of ethics codes." However, he added, "Since ethics codes vary in different locales, who could reasonably claim it is wrong?"

Undeterred, when given his five minutes to question the scholar, Congressman Lenard Hill berated Dr. Arnold for claiming that Adam's wife Eve originated plagiarism at the beginning of time when she quoted the snake that enticed her to eat the forbidden fruit. He excitedly shouted, "This was not plagiarism. Eve was giving testimony. Besides, plagiarism is quoting someone's idea without naming the person. She named the snake. You're mistaken."

Dr. Arnold smiled and explained, "The Bible reveals that Eve named the snake in her plagiarism only because she felt the need to inform God that one of his creatures needed punishment. This was a noble deed. Eve deserves credit for diverging from strict plagiarism to perform a good deed."

Dr. Arnold continued, "The term 'plagiarism' comes from the Latin word for 'kidnapper' and is thought to be a form of theft, a breach of honesty. This is the common anti-plagiarism notion, but not ours in 'Plagiarism International.' We recognize that ideas belong to everyone, not just the first person who thought of them. The US Constitution recognizes 'free speech.' Our lawyers are certain it includes 'free thoughts.' A thought should not be buried in a grave with the ancient person who first developed it. It must be revived, adopted by a living person, and given the name of the individual who heroically resurrected the thought for the enjoyment of humankind."

Democratic and Republican congressmen and women lined up after Dr. Arnold's presentation and praised him. Lenard Hill was shunned.

Chapter Thirteen
Reincarnation

Jake was sure he had found proof of reincarnation as a fact. He reasoned, "My wife is so wonderful that she must be a gift from God to me, but why would God think I am worthy of such a gift? It must be because I did something wonderful to deserve her, yet I never did such a thing. It must be that I did it in a former life. This proves that reincarnation is a fact."

Another man explained reincarnation to his wife by saying, "After you die, you return in a different condition." When she replied that she wanted to return as a cow, he realized that she wasn't listening to him.

A man who believed in reincarnation tried to get paid for a back injury from an insurance company that also believed as he did. The company refused to pay, saying he had a preexisting condition.

A father and son discussed conflicting views about reincarnation when the son told his dad, "When I was your age, I also did not believe in reincarnation."

POINT TO PONDER

Does a life based on a belief that there is life after death cause believers to achieve all they can be while they are alive and prompt them to improve others and all that exists on Earth?

Or does belief in life after death excuse believers when behaving badly by blaming who they were in a previous life?

Chapter Fourteen
Is Reincarnation a Fact, a Lie, or a Truth?

Many people are convinced that reincarnation, called *gilgul* in Hebrew, is an accepted fact since ancient times. Reincarnation is the belief that when people die, they are transferred into a new body in their next life. This is not true about Judaism. *Gilgul* entered Judaism for some mystical-minded Jews only in the Middle Ages.

I will summarize some scholarly ideas about the Jewish view and follow them with my thoughts.

In her 2001 PhD thesis, *The Soul and Afterlife in Jewish Mysticism and Gnosticism*, Dr. Dina Ripsman Eylon gives us the origin of the notion of reincarnation in Judaism.

She informs us that the twelfth-century kabbalistic work *Sefer Bahir*, which literally means "Book of Clarity," is the first Jewish book that introduces the theory of reincarnation as a Jewish theological theory. It is an anonymous mystical work attributed to a first-century rabbinic sage Nehunya ben HaKanah because it begins with the words, "Rabbi Nehunya ben HaKanah said." It is also known as the Midrash of Rabbi Nehunya ben HaKanah.

The book explains the mystical significance of many items including biblical verses, the shapes of Hebrew letters, biblical cantillation signs, and vowel points added to the letters. It also mentions the earlier mystic book *Sefer Yetzirah*, the use of sacred names in magic, and introduces the idea of reincarnation.

Gershom Scholem, the renowned scholar of Jewish mysticism, dated *Bahir*'s composition to 1176 and said that the book enormously impacted Jewish thought, although not every scholar agrees with his dating of *Bahir*. There is a discrepancy of when the work is dated. Although no one dates it earlier than 1176, some date it later, and assert that the doctrine of reincarnation was not in the original version of *Bahir*. They claim that different publishers changed and added to the original text, even frequently. What is certain, is that while other religions and cultures may have accepted the notion of reincarnation as a fact, Judaism did so only when it was introduced in *Bahir*. There is no hint of it in the Torah, Talmuds, and early Midrashim.

Rational thinking Jews rejected the idea that humans lived former lives. Mystical thinkers such as the Greek Plato (circa 428–347 BCE) and the Jewish Nachmanides (1194–1270) accepted it. However, the Greek Aristotle (384–322 BCE) and the Jewish Maimonides (1138–1204) rebuffed the idea.

Dr. Eylon recognizes that Jews may have taken the concept of reincarnation from non-Jews. She adds that some Jews were able to accept the notion because they had already adopted the idea that souls exist, a belief also not in the Hebrew Bible. Philo (25 BCE–50 CE) was the first Jewish philosopher to introduce the suggestion that there is such a thing as a soul that exists separate from the body. It contains the intellect and personality of a person. Platonic theories influenced him. He considered the soul to be eternal. However, he did not have the belief in reincarnation. The soul remained somewhere in limbo until the messianic age when it would be revived.

Neither Aristotle nor Maimonides concluded that there is a soul. Aristotle wrote that the intellect was part of the body. Nothing on earth disappears, but is often transformed into something else. The body is transformed and absorbed into the world, but the intellect goes elsewhere. Maimonides agreed with him.

WHY DID MANY PEOPLE ACCEPT THAT REINCARNATION HAPPENS?
We do not know. However, it is most likely caused by human imperfections and the hope that one can improve in another life.

Most people know little about their religion. Those who know something only remember what they learned in Sunday School, which consists of several afternoon classes held in churches or synagogues for a few hours a week. These lessons are what children can absorb, not the truth adults should know.

Many learned about their religion by listening to radio or TV preachers who were more interested in their money than in their education or to rabbis who presented interesting but untrue homiletical midrashim in their sermons as facts.

Others saw a bearded, saintly-looking man saying whatever he claimed, which others took as his wisdom simply because of his beard or presumed piety. Still others accepted teachings that were not rational, such as, "You need to take a leap of faith," and took no time to interpret it as, "If you find a religious thought to be illogical, you should accept it anyway."

Then there are others who swallowed the belief that people are resurrected from one body to another and never die because it makes them, like many other people who dislike, or fear the thought that there is no life after death, feel better. They will exist even after they die, albeit in a different body, without recollecting the past.

Additionally, resurrection is a convenient explanation of why righteous people suffer. They are punished for misdeeds they committed in a prior life. It also explains why many evil people prosper. They are rewarded for the good they did in a former life.

Therefore, for many rational people, reincarnation is untrue.

Chapter Fifteen
Beliefs

A man who fervently "believed" that a prayer would aid his deceased mother, drove to the cemetery and searched for a rabbi to say a blessing to help his dead mom. He saw a rabbi near a couple praying over the couple's parent's grave. When the couple left, he approached the rabbi and asked if he would pray over his mom's grave.

"Certainly," the rabbi replied. "Would you want it with or without a beard?"

Surprised, but preferring the most pious, he responded, "With a beard."

Whereupon, the rabbi reached into his pocket, drew out a beard, attached it to his chin, and said the prayer to aid the man's mom.

Amazingly, many people "believe" that an apple caused Adam and Eve to be banished from the Garden of Eden when the Bible does not specifically mention an apple. Any reader of the Bible would know it was simply a fruit from the tree of knowledge that Eve gave to Adam.

A father encouraged his son to marry a girl with the same "beliefs" as their family. He responded, "You really want me to marry a woman who thinks I'm a schmuck?"

Doctors "practice" medicine because they are not perfect. They have a lot to learn.

Amazingly, people believe things that are not true. According to "Interesting Facts" on the internet, George Washington did not chop down a cherry tree, Thomas Edison did not invent the light bulb, Marie Antoinette did not say, "Let them eat cake," William Tell did not shoot an apple off of his son's head, and Paul Revere never yelled, "The British are coming."

POINT TO PONDER

The more we learn, the more we know, and the more we know the more we realize how much more there is to learn.

Chapter Sixteen
My List of Three Basic Principles of Judaism

Many Jewish sages offered their list of what they considered the basic principles of Judaism. Maimonides lists thirteen. However, other scholars had different lists. For example, Shem Tov ben Joseph Falaquera (c. 1220–90) identifies seven principles in one of his books and six in another, but some overlap, and these do not align with those of Maimonides.[1] Shimon ben Tzemach Duran (1361–1444) in his *Ohev Mishpat*, and Joseph Albo (fifteenth century) in *Sefer Ha-Ikkarim*, list only three basic Jewish ideas that they feel every Jew must hold in order not to be considered a heretic. Hasdai Crescas (1340–1410) in *Or Ha-Shem*, writes of six cornerstones of faith that he is convinced are the foundation of the Torah. David ben Yom Tov ibn Bilia (fourteenth century) lists twenty-six principles of faith in his *Yesodot ha-Maskil*.[2] Don Isaac Abarbanel

---

1. Dr. Raphael Jospe, *Torah and Sophia: The Life and Thought of Shem Tov Ibn Falaquera*. Cincinnati, OH: Hebrew Union College Press, 1988, 98, 99.
2. David ben Yom Tov ibn Bilia, *Yesodot ha-Maskil*.
   1. The existence of incorporeal intellects;
   2. The creation of the world;
   3. The existence of a future life;
   4. Emanation of the soul from God;
   5. The soul's existence through its own substance and its self-consciousness;
   6. Its existence independent of the body it subsequently occupies;
   7. Retribution of the soul;
   8. Perdition of the souls of the wicked;
   9. Superiority of the Mosaic law over philosophy;
   10. The presence of an esoteric as well as an exoteric meaning in Holy Scripture;
   11. Inadmissibility of emendations of the Torah;
   12. The reward of the fulfilment of the divine precepts implied in the precepts themselves;
   13. The inadequacy of ceremonial laws alone for the realization of human perfection.
   These, together with the thirteen articles of Maimonides, make twenty-six, the numerical value of the Tetragrammaton.

38 · HUMOROUS, SERIOUS, AND THOUGHTFUL IDEAS

(1437–1508) in *Rosh Amanah* has the largest number. He argues that each of the 613 Torah commandments is a fundamental concept of Judaism.

Before Maimonides and the other rabbis mentioned above, the Torah in Deuteronomy 16:20 demanded, "Justice, justice is what you must pursue." Then the biblical prophet Micah (740–670 BCE) wrote in his book in 6:8, "What does the Lord require of you? Act justly, love mercy, and walk humbly with your God." Also, Rabbi Akiva, who was murdered by the Romans in 135 CE, wrote that there is one fundamental principle of the Torah. It is "Love your neighbor as yourself" in Leviticus 19:18. The Torah also states this in different words thirty-six times: "You must love the stranger." This, of course, includes non-Jews. Before Akiva, Hillel (just before and just after the onset of the Common Era) interpreted Leviticus 19:18 and said, "What is hateful to you, do not do to your fellow man: this is the whole Law; the rest is mere commentary" (Babylonian Talmud, *Shabbat* 31a). Ben Azzai, a student of Rabbi Akiva, disagreed with him. He said that a more significant verse is Genesis 6:1. "This is the book of the generations of man (Adam). In the day God created man, He made him in the likeness of God." He emphasized that God created every human, and each is equal.

I think all the scholars mentioned in the former paragraph would agree that the Torah included their wording in Leviticus 19:18, "Act with others as you want them to act toward you."

Other rabbis and Torah scholars dispute Maimonides' thirteen principles as essentials for rational thinkers, but rather as lists of ideas for people not very educated to believe. I agree with this last understanding.

Here is my list of three.

TREAT EVERYONE PROPERLY

I agree with the Torah, Hillel, Akiva, Ben Azzai, and others that the first basic principle is to treat others as you want them to treat you. I think this is also what Micah had in mind.

WE MUST BE RATIONAL

We should avoid relying on beliefs and faith and, instead, use our intellect and think. Beliefs are ideas taught to people who are unable to think. Aristotle said the intellect is what distinguishes us from plants and animals. Maimonides said it is the "image of God" mentioned in Genesis. This does not mean avoiding

Torah mandates. The Torah is filled with wisdom that we will see if we interpret it rationally. We should remember that Exodus 33:18–23 teaches that we can know nothing about God other than what God created or formed. This is nature and its laws. Wisdom requires us to learn science, which analyzes what God created or formed. As we learn from the Greek philosopher Socrates, we should remember that humans cannot know everything.

OBSERVE THE SABBATH

People mistakenly believe that Rosh Hashana and Yom Kippur are the year's holiest days. Many attend synagogues only during these holidays, which are not mentioned in the Torah. The days, weeks, and even the year after this attendance are no different than before their attendance. Others are scrupulous about attending family Seders on Passover, but neglect other ways to honor family.

The primary holy day in Judaism is Shabbat. My father, Rabbi Dr. Nathan Drazin taught that the more you keep Shabbat, the more Shabbat keeps you. We must observe Shabbat actively and properly. We must not focus foolishly on what we should refrain from doing. Only then can we understand that to know God means understanding what God created. We will realize what is important in life by treating everybody and everything, even animals and inanimate objects, as they want and should be treated. Then we will learn how to enjoy life. Shabbat improves individuals and society. It is a foretaste of paradise.

Chapter Seventeen
Two Torah Messages Often Missed

Many people recognize that the Five Books of Moses, the Torah, contain multiple examples of behaviors that we should learn and emulate. However, they fail to notice that every person mentioned in the Torah has misbehaved, and they agonize over misbehaving children. For instance:

EVEN THE BEST HUMANS MISBEHAVE

The Torah criticizes Adam and Eve, the first humans and examples to their descendants, for eating a forbidden fruit.

Nachmanides berates Abraham for lying about Sarah, his wife, presenting her as his sister in order to save his life.

Isaac, the second of the three patriarchs, exemplars of Judaism, favored Esau instead of Jacob.

Jacob, the third and last patriarch, rounds out the list by showing that he, too, misbehaved. First, he steals Isaac's blessing intended for Esau the firstborn, and then by his own preference for Joseph. This caused family jealousy, the Israelites being enslaved in Egypt for over a century, and many deaths.

Not only the three patriarchs, but even their wives, the four matriarchs, misbehaved. Each acted contrary to their husband's wishes. Abraham's wife Sarah forced Abraham to evict his son Ishmael, whom he loved. Rebecca, Isaac's wife, tricked her husband into blessing the son she favored rather than the son Isaac preferred. Jacob's two wives, Rachel and Leah, conspired together to deceive Jacob and cause him to marry Leah first rather than his beloved Rachel, resulting in Jacob having to work for seven years before he was allowed to wed Rachel.

Moses, "our teacher," blasted the Israelites just before he was to take them into Canaan. God saw that this showed Moses was no longer the man to lead the

Israelites into Canaan, and after telling him to appoint Joshua as his successor, God killed him.

Moses' brother Aaron built a golden calf for the Israelites to worship when Moses was absent. It resulted in over a thousand people being killed.

CHILDREN OF WORTHY PARENTS REJECT THE WAYS OF THEIR PARENTS

Two of Aaron's sons, who were priests, brought unauthorized fire on the altar and were killed for what they did (Leviticus 10:1).

"Our teacher" and "lawgiver" Moses' grandson and descendants worshipped idols. This is stated in Judges 18:30, "There [in the city formerly called Laish] the Danites set up for themselves the idol, and Jonathan son of Gershom, the son of Moses, and his sons were priests for the tribe of Dan until the time of the captivity of the land." (The Masorites placed the letter *nun* above the name Moses, hoping to mislead people from realizing the embarrassing phenomenon that Moses' descendants rejected God and would read Monases rather than Moses.)

LESSONS TO LEARN FROM BEHAVIOR IN THE HEBREW BIBLE

The Torah wants us to know that all people, even the best among us, are not perfect. So, if we do wrong, we should learn from our mistakes, resolve to change, and develop habits that train us to be better. These are the steps suggested by Maimonides.

- We must be ever vigilant. There are many stories of people who behaved bravely and praiseworthily until their old age when they did wrong. An example is Moses' sister Miriam, who saved his life shortly after his birth, but eighty years later criticized him, for which God struck her with leprosy.
- In contrast, there are tales of wrongdoers who performed worthy acts in later life. An example is Reish Lakish (circa 200–275), who was a thief, but later became one of the two most learned rabbis of his generation when he joined with his brother-in-law Rabbi Yochanan ben Nappaha (circa 180–279). Another is Rabbi Akiva, an ignorant shepherd until his wife persuaded him to attend school when he was forty, ultimately becoming the teacher of millions.

Danya Ruttenberg in her book, *On Repentance and Repair: Making Amends in an Apologetic World*, lists five Maimonidean principles of repentance.

1. Naming and owning harm
2. Starting to change/transformation
3. Restitution and accepting consequences
4. Apology
5. Making different choices

We should not despair if our children do not do what we taught them. Parents do not have total control over children and should not feel guilty. We are only expected to do all that is reasonable.

Chapter Eighteen
The Truth about Facts and Jokes

TRUTHS

Maimonides famously taught in his *Guide for the Perplexed*, "The truth is the truth no matter what its source," and told readers he based much of his philosophy on the writings of the Greek pagan Aristotle.

Jewish philosophy, such as the writings of Maimonides, begins with facts established by science or reason and then interprets the Bible using those facts. In contrast, Jewish theology, such as the writings of Saadiah Gaon, starts with an understanding of what the Bible teaches and then interprets the world and philosophy according to the Bible.

For instance, Maimonides drew from Aristotelian philosophy that it is possible that matter coexisted with God for eternity. Therefore, he interpreted the introduction to the Bible, Genesis 1:1 and 2, differently than most translators. The two verses state, "In the beginning God *bara* (a Hebrew word generally translated 'created') the heaven and the earth. And the earth was *tohu vavohu* (Hebrew words of uncertain meaning, usually translated 'without form')...."[1] He wrote in his *Guide* that *bara* could mean "formed" and *tohu vavohu* "unformed matter."

In contrast, while Maimonides and other rationalists understood that the *kavod* (translated, "glory of God") in Exodus 40:34–38 meant a human feeling

---

1. Rashi and Abraham ibn Ezra "treat it as a temporal clause, subordinate to verse 3...(and) the verse will read: In the beginning of God's creating the heavens and the earth...." The quote is from *The International Critical Commentary, A Critical and Exegetical Commentary on Genesis* by John Skinner, Charles Scribner's Sons, 1910, 12. It was part of a set of books that my father, Rabbi Dr. Nathan Drazin, owned.

46 · HUMOROUS, SERIOUS, AND THOUGHTFUL IDEAS

that God was present, Saadiah Gaon accepted the traditional literal interpretation of the term, which states that God created a unique being to appear in the Tabernacle.[2]

Maimonides criticized Saadiah Gaon for his interpretation, warning that it smacked of polytheism. Indeed, in post-biblical times. Jews began to call the *kavod* the Shechinah, and many Jews today think the Shechinah is a divine being. There is a saying attributed to various people such as Mark Twain, Jonathan Swift, and Winston Churchill, "A lie gets halfway around the world before the truth has a chance to get its pants on."

We cannot expect to find truth from people whose understanding is warped with enthusiasm.

JOKES

Conan O'Brien joked, "I'm getting older. I used to be able to run a four-minute mile, bench press 380 pounds, and tell the truth."

A snake walks into a bar. The bartender says, "How did you do that?"

I haven't owned a watch for I don't know how long.

---

2. The word "glory" appears 376 times in the Hebrew Bible and 230 in the New Testament.

Chapter Nineteen
The Truth Is the Truth, No Matter What Its Source

Charles H. Freundlich's book *Together Again* is wonderful. Of only about half a dozen rabbis whose synagogues I would want to visit, Rabbi Freundlich's is high on my list. If only I were younger and lived where he was a rabbi, I would rush on Shabbat mornings to his synagogue to hear his sermons, and on weekday nights to listen to his lectures. I have read, reviewed, praised, and enjoyed each of his previous books, now adding this one to his ever-growing list of publications.

The first of his seven tales is the true story of his early life. It is very well-written and emotional, and reflects his warm personality. The following six are fictitious and address significant issues that confront Judaism. Freundlich addresses them with clarity, intelligence, sympathy, and consideration. They are fascinating, eye-opening, and thought-provoking.

The second tale focuses on the problem of the ultra-orthodox in Israel not participating in aiding the country and are living off of the country's charity. The third looks at how to solve family problems. The fourth examines whether the study of the Talmud is taught improperly. (I think it is.) The fifth analyses parents reuniting with children who were angry with them. The sixth deals with how to interact with people with seemingly untraditional ideas. The last shows that happiness can be found in the most unlikely places, even in the Western movie *Shane* and the comedy *Groundhog Day*. For the truth is the truth, no matter what its source.

Chapter Twenty
Crowd Jokes

The cemetery is so crowded that people are dying to get in.

A man shot into a crowd at the train station and didn't hit one person. When questioned by the police about why he missed, someone said, "Because he is gay. He can't shoot straight."

A man tossed a ball into the crowd as baseball players did at ball games and was surprised the trend does not extend to bowling balls.

God visits many nations to teach His Torah. He gets to Egypt and asks the Egyptians, "Will you take my commandments?" They say, "No."

He arrives in Syria and asks, "Will you follow my commandments?" And they answer, "No."

He gets to Israel and asks, "Will you accept my commandments?" The crowd questions, "How much do they cost?"

God replies, "They're free."

The crowd shouts back, "We'll take ten!"

Chapter Twenty-One
The Crowd Instinct and Power

Elias Canetti (1905–1994) was a Jewish German-language writer born in Ruse, Bulgaria. His family moved to England, where his father died in 1912. His mother took their three sons back to Europe and settled in Vienna. In 1981, her son Elias was awarded the Nobel Prize in Literature for "writings marked by a broad outlook, a wealth of ideas, and artistic power."

Canetti wrote in his book *The Memoirs of Elias Canetti*, "I realized that there is such a thing as a crowd instinct, which is always in conflict with the personality instinct, and that the struggle between the two of them can explain the course of human history." This idea became central to his life. It is the focus of his book *Crowds and Power*. He defined "crowd instinct" as an instinctive desire to be part of a crowd, to even dissolve one's personality into a large mass of people. It often happens in mass rallies where impassioned orators fire up their audience, and at rock concerts where young and old fans lose themselves in their wild admiration of the singers and their music.

The opposite of crowd instinct is "personality instinct." We occasionally agree with crowds, but want to retain our ideas and values. We know from our knowledge of history that crowds have often become dangerous. Demagogues passed on false information, controlled the population, and often drove them to do terrible acts, including murder.

In *Crowds and Power*, Canetti revolutionizes our analyses of politics and history. He shows many examples of the pathology of crowds in various countries and religions, and he informs us of such mundane things as how a ruler's digestion can affect his power. He emphasizes that it takes people with strong personal instincts and a clear understanding of their ideas and values who can overcome the phenomenal power of the crowd instinct. This could help us explain the rise of antisemitism around the world today and the sizable percentage of Americans who overlook the bestialities committed by Hamas on October 7, 2023, and protest blindly in favor of Hamas, violently destroying property during their protests.

He describes many kinds of crowds. Each is different with distinct behaviors and motivations. He reveals the sociology and psychology of each of them. Among the crowds he mentions they might be open, closed, crowds as rings, invisible, baiting, flight, prohibition, reversal, feast, double men and women crowds, double living and dead crowds, war crowds, and crowd crystals.

There are also many smaller groupings, each, as with the crowds, with distinct behaviors and motives. He calls the smaller groups packs. There are hunting packs, war packs, lamenting packs, increase packs, communion packs, and inward and tranquil packs.

Canetti discusses much about crowds and packs. These include their history, their appearance in legends, how they transform, and how they appear in Islam, Christianity, and Judaism.

This is offered to us in easy-to-read language, with many examples and details in the first 200 pages of this thought-provoking masterpiece. He follows the discussion of crowds and packs until page 495 with a brilliant discussion of power, its elements, its aspects, its survivors, details about commands, and transformation. As with crowds and packs, he fills his pages with fascinating details and examples from many cultures and history.

Canetti also tells us that humans not only learned a lot by observing how animals act, but they also learned many valuable things by looking at their bodies. For example, "the feel of the hand of authority on his shoulder is usually enough to make a man give himself up without having to be actually seized. He cowers and goes quietly." Humans learned much by thinking about their teeth. "The way they are arranged in rows and their shining smoothness are quite different from anything else in the body." It taught humans about order, architecture, protection, dangers, smooth surfaces, and more. The nail on the index finger for instance taught people about knives, and spears. The thumb led to thinking about grasping the bow for arrows. The movement of the fingers led to how to weave and other arts. Even thinking about how one eats led people to invent new objects and goals.

Just as Sigmund Freud revolutionized psychology with need-to-know information written in very readable and entertaining language, Elias Canetti has done the same by revealing the truths about crowds and power.

Chapter Twenty-Two
Meat-Eater Jokes

Pessimists are like German vegetarians. They fear the wurst.

People who don't eat meat are called vegetarians, but what are people who don't eat vegetables called? Constipated.

What do you call a dog with a fever? Hot dog.

Joe says at the hot dog stand, "Can I get a jumbo sausage?" The hot dog guy replies: "Sure. Won't be long." Joe: "In that case, can I have two?"

A hot dog and a hamburger enter a bar. The bartender immediately yells, "I'm sorry, we don't serve food here."

Children were lined up in the school cafeteria for lunch. They saw a large tray of hot dogs and a sign that said, "Take only one. God is watching." A large pile of chocolate chip cookies was at the end of the line. One child whispered to his buddy, "Take all you want. God is watching the hot dogs."

Chapter Twenty-Three
Michael's Trip to Heaven

The wind blew fiercely with hurricane force. His roof was torn from his house and landed a block away where the air was calm. The rain flooded down like knives. It landed on his head and eyes. Lightning struck only him. It hit his legs, then his arms, and it waited some ten minutes while he rolled in pain. Then it struck his heart, and he rose to Heaven.

Six angels were at the gate. They stood somber, even embarrassed. The tallest came forward, reached out his hand to welcome him, and said, "We had no part in this, Michael. We are sorry to see you."

Abraham and Moses, who generally welcomed the righteous, were also too embarrassed to appear.

There were no welcome signs. Souls stood on the sidelines to watch the entrance, but were silent.

The three forces attacked the movers, the angels assigned to bring the list of good and bad deeds to Heaven in boxes for review. Rain blotted the list of Michael's good deeds, so they were undecipherable. Wind blew sheets to the burning cauldron of Hell. Lightning burned out words in the good list, turning the remaining sentences into accusations.

They determined that Michael would end up in Hell. He would now be God's scapegoat.

This was war.

"We're tired of being blamed for evil happenings on earth," Hurricane winds roared. "Why were we the scapegoats?" shouted flooding Rains. "Let beloved Michael bear the brunt and burn from the abuse," Lightning screamed with fury.

Michael stood at Heaven's Gate dumbfounded. Why was he involved?

He was a simple man, unlearned. He had left the weekend synagogue school when his dad died, and his mom wanted him to work to support her and his two sisters. He had only three weekend years of learning. If he were tested about God and religion, he would fail. He couldn't write a sensible sentence. Yet, unknown to him, God loved him. No one in Heaven or Earth could explain this love. And this added to the fury of the three warriors. Why was he loved? He did nothing for God. At the same time, they did what God demanded and ignored the blame cast upon them for centuries! Enough was enough. They demanded justice.

They hired an attorney and filed suit against God, whom they called a well-meaning, benevolent dictator. Although it caused quite a racket in Heaven, God allowed it.

In their document of charges, they mocked Michael, whose name in Hebrew means, "Who is like God!" They wrote, "Is God so superior? Is God without any fault? We will show that this is untrue."

The document quoted the Greek philosopher Epicurus (341–270 BCE), a wise teacher whose wisdom reflects the truth. He recognized that people need pleasure and made it a basis for his egoistic hedonism. He said, "The only thing that is intrinsically valuable is one's pleasure; anything else that has value is valuable merely as a means to securing pleasure for oneself." They asked, "Is all the evil and harm on earth pleasurable? Is it proper? Is this sensible leadership?"

They reminded the court that God agreed with Epicurus when the philosopher said he valued learning. Epicurus said, "Let no one be slow to seek wisdom when he is young nor weary in search of it when he has grown old. For no age is too early or too late for the health of the soul." "How," they asked, "can one who values learning allow so much pain that detracts people from learning?"

"God," they argued, "also agreed with the sage when he recognized that while he was blessed with wisdom, most people were not. Epicurus said, "I never desired to please the rabble. What pleased them, I did not learn, and what I knew was far removed from their understanding." "How," the plaintiffs asked again, "can a benevolent creator create people with insufficient sense?"

Their lawyer pounded the podium in his summary. "Wasn't Epicurus correct in criticizing God when he became frustrated about the existence of evil and harm in this world and found no solution to the problem? He said, 'Is God willing to prevent evil but not able? Then, he is not omnipotent. Is he able but not willing? Then, he is malevolent. Is he both able and willing? Then, whence cometh evil? Is he neither able nor willing? Then, why call him God?'" And he concluded with the words, "If this court is unable to answer Epicurus' analysis, shouldn't this court find God guilty?"

Nothing further about this ancient trial has been found despite the searches of many scholars. What is significant is that since the trial, no word has been heard from God. Was God found guilty and imprisoned?

This fictional tale I invented reflects the view of people who are atheists, such as the British biologist Richard Dawkins (born 1941). In his book, *The God Delusion* he insists that a supernatural creator called God does not exist. It is a delusion, a persistent false belief held in the face of strong contradictory evidence.

This is not acceptable to me as I do not see evidence that God does not exist. While I lack irrebuttable evidence proving God exists, I think that the beauties and marvels of this world support the idea that there was and is a superior something that created or formed it.

I partially agree with his other statements. He explains why he believes science is more important than religion. He says he accepts that things may be far grander and more incomprehensible than we can imagine. He adds that his eyes are constantly wide open to the extraordinary fact of existence. But, "I am against religion because it teaches us to be satisfied with not understanding the world." It encourages religious people not to look for other answers. It tells people to believe God did and does all things, and it is unreligious to look or find another theory or answer.

His view that religion is not as important as science is an over generalization, but he is correct in criticizing people who shun science. Like religion, science tries to teach proper behavior that will improve everything on earth.

Chapter Twenty-four
A Possible Solution to Why There Is Evil

I will explain why there is evil in this world. God did what is sensible. The world is, as the Hebrew Bible states, "Good." It gives people free will. Humans cause evil in three ways.

THE WORLD IS CREATED WITH DUALITY
Opposites are generally two sides of the same thing. For example, love and hate are related. They are two ends of the same emotion. Love can lead to hate and vice versa. It is the cause of many divorces when married couples fail to realize they moved from one end of their feeling to the other. Even when people remember this fact, they forget they can help themselves by moving from one extreme on the continuum to the other.

This fact of nature was recognized in ancient times. While non-existent in Greek theology, Janus was seen as having two faces in Roman theology. He was the god of doors, gates, and transitions. He was the middle ground between dualities such as life and death, beginning and end, youth and adulthood, rural and urban, and barbarism and civilization. Romans turned to this god to ensure that their transition from one end of life's pole to another, such as war to peace, was successful.

This fact of nature may explain why many people fail to understand why there is evil in this world. They do not see that evil is part of the duality of good and evil. Winds and hurricanes can be harmful, but they also clean the air. Lightning can cause harm, but it also does good. Rain causes floods, irrigates the ground, and gives us water. The challenge is to learn how to use and balance these forces. I do not know how God thinks; perhaps He thought as follows: I can create humans who will always have an easy life, where people always enjoy pleasures, a life without any problems. But if I did so, people would be senseless puppets, just senseless mechanical robots.

Instead of making puppets, God created a world with duality where people are challenged to grow in their thinking and behavior. Those who pay attention will find the world given to them is fascinating. They will recognize the challenges and will enjoy engaging in them. They will seek to improve themselves and all creation.

This understanding that the world was created with duality and with challenges to humans to work to bring matters to the right side of a continuum is consistent with the way the Torah teaches its lessons. The Hebrew Bible, the Torah, was written for the generation to which it was given to help people live a good life. It is filled with hints on how the presented laws can be changed. For example, the Torah allowed sacrifices, slavery, punishment by an eye for an eye, and taking a female captive during a war. Still, it always sets boundaries and hints to encourage change. A close reading of the Torah reveals that it opposes these things and desires the opposite.

Thus, the world is not filled with evil per se. It is filled with duality and challenges, with free will and promptings for humans to face challenges, learn how to behave with them, enjoy the learning, and use better behavior to improve individuals and all God made available.

IT IS IMPOSSIBLE TO CREATE A PERFECT LAW

It must also be understood that creating a perfect law or rule that will never hurt anyone is impossible. Circumstances will arise when a statute or rule that is good for society will harm individuals. This is part of nature. If laws always resulted in good, there would be no free will. This is why Maimonides differentiated morality from rationality in his *Guide for the Perplexed* 1:2. Morality is not the truth. Morality is the best idea applicable at certain times in certain localities for the best situation for humans. An excellent moral law is not crossing a street against a red light. But there are occasions when it makes good sense to do so, as when one is pursued by a person who wants to kill you. An intelligent person would not follow the moral law. Maimonides, as did Nietzsche in later times, suggested that the intelligent man, whom Nietzsche called the *Übermensch*, would act according to reason.

Humans who fail to use reason create evil.

IF IT IS EASY, IT IS PROBABLY WRONG

Clearly, acting according to the prior understanding is not easy. People fail to realize that if a thing is easy, it is probably wrong. When they take the easy approach, they are furthering evil.

In short, the world is good. It is designed to give humans free will. Humans have produced evil because they have not acted properly.

Chapter Twenty-Five
The History of Shoes and Clothing

SOCKS

Archeologists found paintings in caves dated around 5000 BCE that show that people during the Stone Age wore socks made from animal skins. The eighth century BCE Greek poet Hesiod wrote that the ancient Greeks wore socks called *piloi*, made from matted animal hair. A study in the Journal of Physiological Anthropology found that young men fell asleep 7.5 minutes faster, slept 32 minutes longer, and woke up 7.5 times less frequently than other young men who slept without wearing socks.[1]

SHOES

The earliest known pair of shoes predate the use of socks. Archeologists suggest that the first humans used them to protect their feet around 8000 BCE. They were made from tree bark. Historians date the first use of shoes made from leather to around 3500 BCE.

The word shoe may have been derived from Proto-Indo-European *skek*, which means to move quickly or jump.

Historians suggest that the Romans were the first to design left and right-foot shoes. Other civilizations did so later independently.

---

1. Yelin Ko and Joo-Young Lee, "Effects of feet warming using bed socks on sleep quality and thermoregulatory responses in a cool environment." *Journal of Physiological Anthropology*, 2018.

HEELS

Some historians say that heels were invented in Persia and designed for wealthy men who wore them to give them additional height. Men stopped wearing heels when women began to wear them in the eighteenth century.

SKIRTS

Skirts have been worn since prehistoric times for men and women in all ancient cultures in the Middle East. Men wore dresses for centuries. Boys stopped wearing skirts about a hundred years ago. They wore dresses until age five, sometimes older. Transitioning to pants was called breeching. Boys were kept in dresses to make potty training easier.

Today, men's clothes are buttoned to the right, while women's are buttoned to the left. Some people claim that the buttons for men were placed on the right to make dueling easier. Since women did not duel, their buttons were left on the left. Other people say it was the fault of men that originated the difference in buttons. It was wealthy women whom their maids dressed. Since most maids were right-handed, having the buttons on the left made it easier for them to button their mistress' dress.

Both ideas, in my view, are unlikely. Not every man dueled. Most of the population was not wealthy, and the women dressed themselves. More likely, the idea was invented by salespeople who wanted to sell more clothing. Manufacturers tried to stop men and women from wearing the same clothes by making them with slight differences, thus selling more of them by virtue of variety.

Chapter Twenty-Six
Ethical Behaviors Concerning Shoes

Many cultures and religions have laws or practices requiring people to remove their shoes on certain occasions.

- Moses was commanded in Exodus 3:5 and Joshua in Joshua 5:15 to remove their shoes when Moses had a revelation from God at a burning bush, and Joshua received instructions from an angel.
- Priests who were descendants of Moses' brother Aaron are told in the Bible to minister barefoot in the Tabernacle.
- The Mishna relates in *Berachot* 9:5 that Jews could not enter the Temple Mount wearing shoes, or with a staff, money belt, or dust on their feet.
- Today, priests in Orthodox synagogues ascend a podium and recite a blessing after they remove their shoes. They do so to remember the practice of the ancient priests.
- (A brief note. Of the question of what helped Jews survive years in the diaspora, the answer is recalling Jewish practices such as the priestly blessing, Shabbat, and the Seder on Passover.)
- The Jewish practice is that mourners mourn their departed at home without leather shoes.
- Similarly, all Jews do not wear leather shoes on the fast days of Yom Kippur and Tisha b'Av.
- While Jews discontinued the practice of praying barefoot in synagogues, Muslims adopted the practice in their mosques.
- In Asia, Eastern Europe, and among some Hawaiians and others, shoes are not worn at home; visitors are expected to remove them before entering these homes.

66 · HUMOROUS, SERIOUS, AND THOUGHTFUL IDEAS

WHY?

- Since ancient times, people recognized two significant things about shoes that caused the abovementioned practices. People saw that walking with shoes accumulated dust, dirt, and other undesirable filth. They did not want this trash brought into their homes and places of worship. They also saw that walking was an active activity and people walked with shoes. For example, Judaism requires Jews to be active and to treat all that God created as they want to be treated themselves. The rabbis emphasized the need for activity in many ways. The root of the Hebrew word for laws, *halachah*, means to walk, go, and move.
- So, the removal of shoes was felt to be a sign of respect. Proper people do not soil another's home, or any holy place.
- Feet and shoes were also seen as a possible threat to others, whereas hands were offered in a handshake to other hands to indicate that the owners were not a threat. Similarly, the removal of shoes when entering a home or holy places showed no intended action, or threat, but rather as a sign of respect.

✳ ✳ ✳

After writing this easy, I posted it on my website. My friend Stephen I. Ternyik sent me the following comment to which I added a bracketed explanation:

Dear Rabbi Israel Drazin! I am in agreement with all your observations. IMO [in my opinion], all our texts mention several ethical behaviors concerning shoes. For example, not wearing shoes while mourning (such as after the destruction of Jerusalem), as a sign of respect is one mentioned behavior. It is also considered important to not boast about one's importance, like Eliezer the Younger did when questioned about his wearing black shoes. On Shabbat, it is advised that one may not go out in a single shoe, likely to avoid mockery and potential violations of carrying items on Shabbat, which is forbidden. However, if one has a wound on the foot, they may wear a single shoe – with the shoe on the wounded foot if shoes are seen mainly for protection, or the shoe on the healthy foot if shoes are seen mainly for comfort. There is also an ethical recommendation about the sequence of putting on shoes: right shoe first, but tying the left shoe first, which shows respect to both the general rule of precedence of the right and the special significance of the left arm where arm tefillin is worn. In times of persecution, people were forbidden from wearing hobnailed sandals on Shabbat, especially in sensitive circumstances, to avoid panic and potential harm to others. On Yom Kippur, it is forbidden to wear shoes, possibly to show humility. However, there is debate whether this applies only to leather shoes or any kind of shoes. These are not all universally applicable today and are often tied to specific cultural or religious contexts. It is important to note that the texts interpret these behaviors within their particular historical, religious, and cultural contexts. Best: Stephen.

Chapter Twenty-Seven
Rashi: Marvelous but Irrational

While many people favor Rashi as their Bible commentator, virtually nothing is known about him. People also fail to realize that Rashi generally does not reveal the true intent of the Bible text.

- All we know about Rabbi Shlomo ben Yitzchak, known as Rashi from Troyes, France, are his writings. There are no known facts about his life, and while much has been written about him, most if not all is legend. It is commonly thought, for example, that he was born in the year 1040, although this is uncertain, and his date of death is 1105, even though the first mention of this date is in a document written about two centuries after the scholar's death. We are told that he made his money by growing vines and bottling wines when there is no evidence that this is true.
- Eli Wiesel recognized this problem in his book *Rashi: A Portrait* and wrote: "Yes, we need imagination in order to write about him." Wiesel tells some of the legends that fascinated Rashi's readers and informs them that they are just legends. Instead of inventing facts about the man, Wiesel relates the history of the time that Rashi lived and reasonably assumes the impact of the persecutions suffered in France must have had upon him.
- Rashi's commentaries are not original ideas. He drew fascinating stories from Midrashim and placed them into his commentary. Midrashim are books that collected fanciful, engaging stories written as parables and teaching aids. These could be enjoyable and sometimes even exciting accounts that for the most part, were not originally intended to be understood as actual history or the true meaning of scriptural passages. However, in the

70 · HUMOROUS, SERIOUS, AND THOUGHTFUL IDEAS

thirteenth century, Rashi and others, such as Nachmanides, took these tales as facts and used them to explain the Bible.

- Thus, for example, Rashi introduced his readers to the delightful midrashic report – not even hinted at in the Torah – that God made Abraham's son Isaac look precisely like him so that slanderers could not claim that Abraham was too old to have children and his wife Sarah must have had her son from the Philistine king Abimelech who had abducted her (Genesis 25:19).

- Another example is that the patriarch Jacob was concerned that his soon-to-be scheming father-in-law Laban would substitute Leah in place of her sister, his beloved Rachel, on their wedding night. Hence, he and Rachel agreed on a code she would mention in the dark, and Jacob would know it was her, but feeling sorry for her sister, Rachel revealed the code to Leah, and Jacob was fooled (Genesis 29:25).

- It is hard to forget stories like these, stories learned as children. What is more, Rashi had a very pleasing writing style. He improved the narratives by rewriting the Midrashim to be more lucid, colorful, and understandable.

- Rashi's grandson, Rashbam (Rabbi Samuel ben Meir, circa 1085–1158), who wrote a rational Bible commentary, rebuked his grandfather for inserting these imaginative, fictional, midrashic explanations into his commentary. He chastised him for not sticking to the plain meaning of the biblical passages.

- In Rashbam's commentary on Genesis 37:1, he told his readers that he upbraided his grandfather for the way he explained the Torah and that Rashi assured him that he agreed with him. Rashi said that if he had years to write new explanations, he would write a book like Rashbam's Commentary.

- In Genesis 49:17, where Rashi states that the verse is referring to the judge Samson, who would not be born for another couple of centuries, Rashbam angrily writes that anyone who thinks that 49:17 is speaking about Samson doesn't know how to understand the Torah. In Deuteronomy 15:18, Scripture mandates that a slave owner give his Hebrew slave gifts when he sets the enslaved person free. The Torah continues: "It should not seem hard to you…because he gave you double the service of a hired man." There are several different interpretations of the term "double." Rashi (based on *Midrash Sifrei*) proposes that Scripture's "double" means that Hebrew slaves work day and night while a hired employee works only during the day. The nighttime work is when the master gives the slave a Canaanite slave so that he can have children from the union that would also belong to him as slaves. Rashbam unabashedly calls this interpretation "foolish" and "vapor." The verse's plain meaning is that the "master" should not feel bad for having paid for the slave twice, first when he purchased the slave, and now when he frees him, he must also give him gifts.

- The eleventh-century rationalist Abraham ibn Ezra, who lived around the same time, wrote mockingly: Rashi states that he translates the Torah according to its plain meaning, and he is correct – one time out of a thousand.

- What prompted Rashi to accept the imaginative tales as the true meaning of the Torah?

- In the second century, two highly respected rabbinical figures argued how the Bible was written and how it should be understood. Rabbi Akiva's ideas accepted by most rabbis, including Rashi and many Midrashim, insisted that the Bible was a divine document in which every word, even every letter, was purposely composed by God to instruct humanity. Since God is all-knowing and infallible, the document He wrote, the Torah, must not have any superfluous words or letters. God said exactly what He meant to say. No more and no less. If a biblical verse seems to repeat itself, the seeming repetition must be saying something that is not in the first phrase.

- His contemporary, Rabbi Ishmael, had an opposite view. He argued that the Bible was composed for people and must have been written in ways people could understand. As people talk, the Torah contains metaphors and other figures of speech that should not be taken literally. Like humans, the Torah has hyperbole and repeats itself for various reasons, including for emphasis.

- While sages like Rashi followed Rabbi Akiva's methodology, people like Saadiah Gaon, Rashbam, ibn Ezra, and Maimonides accepted Rabbi Ishmael's approach.

- Once Rashi's approach to Torah is understood, why he wrote what he did becomes clear. He saw words in the Torah that seemed superfluous to him, and felt obliged to explain the verse using Rabbi Akiva's methodology.

- For example, in Deuteronomy 13:5, the Torah states that the Israelites should serve God and cleave to Him. Rabbi Ishmael would see these two statements expressing a single idea: worship God. However, following their methodology, *Midrash Sifrei* and Rashi understood the Bible speaking

72 · HUMOROUS, SERIOUS, AND THOUGHTFUL IDEAS

about two acts. The first means serving God in His Temple; the second is to behave appropriately outside the Temple in daily life.

- Ibn Ezra, to cite another example, following the methodology of Rabbi Ishmael, notes that Deuteronomy 13:6 mentions that the Israelites were both "freed" and "redeemed" and states that the Torah is speaking of a single act. Still, the Torah uses the two verbs to strengthen its argument. *Sifrei* and Rashi, following the way of Rabbi Akiva, understand the verse to say that even if God only "freed" you, it would have been sufficient reason to obey Him; now that He also "redeemed" you, how much more are you obligated to follow Him.

- Although reading Rashi's comments is interesting and entertaining, readers need to know what prompted him to make a remark. Most scholars recognize that Scripture does not hint at what Rashi felt he had to read into the verse and what he surmises about historical events that never occurred.

- Basing his commentaries on imaginative tales is not the only thing we need to know about Rashi.

- Like virtually all of his contemporaries, Jew or non-Jew, Rashi was convinced that the world is filled with angels that people could turn to for assistance, and demons who hovered around them to entice them.

- His world was also ruled by astrological forces threatening the ancient Israelites, such as in Exodus 10:10 when Pharaoh warned Moses that if he took the Israelites from Egypt, he would face the consequences of *ra*. Rashi states that *ra* is a destructive astral force.

- Rashi was convinced that God rewards people for the good that they do. Suppose they have no immediate need for the reward. In that case, it can be stored, as if placed in a bank account and used by future generations, even if the future people do not deserve it themselves – a concept he and many other rabbis called *zechut avot* (ancestral merit).

- These views are not explicit in the Bible, but are mentioned by some rabbis in the Talmuds and the Midrashim, and Rashi incorporates them into his Bible commentary. For example, he introduces most of them into his elaborate interpretation of Genesis 22 when Abraham leads his son Isaac to be sacrificed.

- The Babylonian Talmud, *Chullin* 105b, and Rashi's commentary to the Babylonian Talmud, *Rosh Hashanah* 28a, write that Jews blow the ram's

RASHI: MARVELOUS BUT IRRATIONAL · 73

horn, the shofar, on the New Year holiday Rosh Hashanah to scare demons and upset their plans to harm Jews.

- Rashi, like many Jews his age, was convinced that God is corporeal and has a body, including hands, feet, and head. Commenting upon Exodus 7:4, "I will lay My hand upon Egypt," he emphasizes that "hand" is not a metaphor for "power," as Maimonides would later say, but "an actual hand to smite them." In Exodus 14:31, where "Israel saw the great hand, what God did to Egypt," he tells the reader that when the Torah speaks of God's "hand," it is *yad mamash*, an "actual hand." He expresses the same view in his commentary to the Babylonian Talmud, *Eruvin* 21a and *Yevamot* 49b, where he refers to God's arm and face. Similarly, in his comment on Genesis 1:26, where the Bible states that man was created in God's image, and where Maimonides is quick to note that this means that God gave humans intelligence, Rashi writes, "image means God's form." So, too, in 1:27, "And God created man in His image," Rashi elaborates, "This means that the form that was established for him (man) is the form of the Creator."

- While Maimonides and many rationalists dismiss the idea that angels exist, believing that the word should be understood figuratively as the natural forces of nature or asserting that if they do live, they do so in an incorporeal form, Rashi insists that a pious person can summon a corporeal angel to serve his everyday needs, act as his courier, deliver a message and return with a report of what he sees. Thus, in Genesis 32:4, according to Rashi, Jacob sends *malachim mamash* (actual angels) as postmen to his brother Esau to appease him.

- In Genesis 19:22, Rashi advances his belief in "fallen angels." God punished these angels because, in a frenzy of hauteur, they took personal credit for the destruction of Sodom and Gomorrah in Genesis 19:13. His interpretation of Genesis 19:22 is based on his opinion that God, like an insecure human, can become angry and offended when someone seeks recognition and praise for what He did.

- In Genesis 6:4, Rashi informs his readers that angels can have sexual intercourse with human females and did so.

- According to Rashi, not only do God, angels, and even demons exist and are corporeal, but they can also drown. Ironically, in his commentary on Genesis 6:19, Noah saved them from extinction in a flood designed to

74 · HUMOROUS, SERIOUS, AND THOUGHTFUL IDEAS

eradicate evil. In the Babylonian Talmud, *Berachot* 6a, Rashi describes the demon: "The feet of a demon are like a rooster's."

- Rashi felt that animals could commit moral wrongs and inanimate objects could make decisions. Commenting on Genesis 6:20, Rashi states that Noah's ark performed a miraculous ethical selection process: it did not allow animals that had corrupted themselves with sexual perversions to enter the ark.

- The Babylonian Talmud, *Pesachim* 112a, warns people from drinking "water from rivers during the night." The Talmud explains that the danger is *sabriri*. Rashbam, reasonably explains that *sabriri* means that polluted water can cause medical problems. However, his grandfather states that *sabriri* is the name of a demon that has the power to inflict the people drinking his water with blindness and may lash out in revenge for being disturbed.

- Eric Lawee is a modern scholar who derides Rashi, like Rashi's grandson Rashbam. He described the views of scholars who "viewed Maimonides and Rashi as symbols of larger alternatives in Judaism and Jewish life. Maimonides was the emblem of rationality in biblical exegesis…. These scholars saw Rashi's diet of *derashot* agreeable to women and children offered up by Rashi's philosophically innocent commentary…evidence of Judaism's abysmal state."[1]

- Lawee gives an example: one ancient who mocked Rashi's commentary on the corruption of "all flesh" in Genesis 6:12 that prompted God to flood the earth and even kill animals because of their sexual immorality. The scholar thought this idea was ridiculous since animals never do anything unnatural in the animal world.

- The same sage wrote that "intelligent people will laugh at the one (Rashi) who says that he (Jacob) blessed him (Pharaoh, in Genesis 47:10) that the Nile should rise before him (since)…the interval when the Nile rises is known and not dependent upon Pharaoh nor any person."

- He also mocked Rashi for saying in his commentary on Genesis 47:19 that the famine ceased as soon as Jacob came to Egypt. If he had this power,

---

1. Eric Lawee, "Maimonides in the Eastern Mediterranean: The Case of Rashi's Resisting Readers," in *Maimonides After 800 Years: Essays on Maimonides and His Influence*, ed. Jay M. Harris (Cambridge, MA: Harvard University Press, 2007), 183–206.

RASHI: MARVELOUS BUT IRRATIONAL · 75

Jacob should have fixed the famine in his home instead of sending his sons to Egypt to beg for food.

- Lawee cites an ancient sage who showed his contempt for Rashi's comment upon Exodus 7:15 that Pharaoh went down to the water, meaning the Nile, "to relieve himself." The scholar writes that this is "*derash* of a dolt, for had he no way to relieve himself in a concealed place such that he had to go down to the river?"
- Lawee summarizes his essay by saying, "These writers ultimately fought a losing battle in trying to defeat the ascendancy of Rashi's commentary." Despite all the criticism, Rashi is the most favored Bible commentator.
- Numbers 13 states that God told Moses to send spies to Canaan to prepare for the entry of the Israelites, but Deuteronomy 1:22 has Moses saying the idea came from the people. The rabbis offer various ideas to reconcile the differences. Relying on *Midrash Tanchuma*, Rashi states the word *lecha* (you) in *shelach lecha* (you send) denotes that if you want to send spies as indicated in Deuteronomy 1, go ahead and do it, but it is not a good idea. However, this is not the plain meaning of the word. Elsewhere, the word *lecha* does not imply "you decide." When God told Abraham to leave his country in Genesis 12, *lech lecha*, God was not saying, "Go if you want to go."
- While Rashi follows Rabbi Akiva's view that God never repeats the same idea, he inconsistently does not try to explain the repetition in Numbers 13:2, "(send) one man, one man."
- Rashi contends that the Torah tells the tale of the spies after the account of Moses' sister Miriam criticizing him because both stories show that people are punished for improper speech.
- He notes the use of the term *anashim* (men) and writes, "Whenever *anashim* is mentioned in the Bible, it denotes distinction, and at that time (when the spies were selected, these men) were honorable. Rashi does not notice that *anashim* is also used to describe evil men.
- Numbers 13 is the first time Joshua is mentioned in the Bible. Verse 16 states that Moses changes his name from Hoshea, which means "save," to Yehoshua, adding the letter *yud*. This results in the name in Hebrew beginning with *yud heh*, a word for God, and the name meaning "God saves."
- The Torah gives no reason for the change. Relying on a midrash, Rashi writes, "He prayed for him. May God deliver you from the counsel of the

76 · HUMOROUS, SERIOUS, AND THOUGHTFUL IDEAS

spies." What defect did Moses see in Joshua that prompted him to pray? Does such a prayer work? Why did Moses send the spies to bring an evil report if he foresaw it?

- Many commentators of the biblical book Numbers criticize Pinchas, the grandson of Moses' brother Aaron, who steps forward when fellow Israelites have been seduced to worship an idol. He kills the principal Israelite offender and the woman with whom he was cohabiting. The critics contend that Pinchas was overzealous. Among other wrongs, he should have asked permission from Moses or a court whether he should murder the pair. Rashi defends Pinchas. In his commentary on 25:7, with no scriptural basis, Rashi contends that Pinchas asked Moses if he had a right to kill Zimri for his behavior, and Moses permitted him.

- Earlier, in 25:6, Rashi imagines that Zimri also came to Moses. He asked if it was forbidden or permissible for him to have sex with Cozbi, a Midianite woman. Zimri added, "If you say she is forbidden, why were you allowed the daughter of Jethro [who was a Midianite]?" Rashi does not include Moses' response and imagines that sex was the issue when the Bible clearly states the problem was idol worship. He makes these suggestions with no basis in the biblical story.

- These examples are only a few out of hundreds of similar ones that show how interesting, yet irrational Rashi's interpretations are because they have no basis in the Torah text.

- Many well-meaning people offer mistaken advice. An example uses Rashi. The ancient rabbis in the Babylonian Talmud, *Berachot* 8 a, b advised Jews to read the Torah twice weekly in the original Hebrew and once in the Aramaic translation called *Targum Onkelos*. I understand they did so because they correctly felt that *Onkelos* was a literal translation.[2] They were saying that we wrote imaginative sermonic midrashim to teach lessons to Jews. While one may gain many ideas from these midrashim, one must understand what the Torah is saying. All of this is found in *Onkelos*. Later rabbis saw that while

---

2. Nachmanides in the thirteenth century was the first to suppose that *Onkelos* contained midrash. Proofs of this and over a hundred errors by Nachmanides on this matter can be found in my book *Nachmanides the Unusual Thinker*. Despite extolling midrash, Rashi, who lived before Nachmanides, never turned to *Onkelos* for midrash, but only to show the Targum containing the plain meaning of the Torah words.

Aramaic was the language people spoke and understood, as English is today, in later days, most people did not understand it. Therefore, they suggested that instead of reading *Onkelos*, one should read Rashi. The rabbis who suggested this misunderstood their predecessors because Rashi was not giving the Torah's plain meaning. He quoted midrashim and indicated that they were more than parables; they were accurate interpretations and intent of the Torah.

Chapter Twenty-Eight
Unknown Facts about the Bible

Let's begin with an example from Exodus 21. It starts with laws concerning a "Hebrew slave." Yet the term is not explained. We are not told how the individual became a slave. It continues with laws on when a man sells his daughter as a slave; a death sentence to a person who kills another; the law of an accidental killing; the rule that holding on to the altar does not protect a murderer; striking a father or mother; kidnapping; insulting parents resulting in the death penalty; "an eye for an eye"; and many more laws. Rabbis changed all of these listed laws. Why?

THE IMPORTANCE OF THE ENTIRE TORAH
- The first set of laws given to the former Israelite slaves was the Decalogue, a brief listing of basic teachings. In the early history of Judaism, the Decalogue was so esteemed by Jews that it was placed in mezuzot in the doorposts of houses and recited daily with morning prayers. Rabbis abandoned this practice in the Babylonian and Jerusalem Talmuds *Berachot* 12a and *Berachot* 1:5. Scholars, such as Aharon Oppenheimer (in "Removing the Decalogue from the 'Shema' and Phylacteries: The Historical Implications," in *The Decalogue in Jewish and Christian Tradition*, ed. Henning Graf Reventlow and Yair Hoffman) explain that they did so because Christians extolled the Decalogue as the only legal authority of the Torah.

WHY WERE THE LAWS CHANGED?
- Remarkably, the first laws in Exodus 21 deal with an Israelite enslaving a fellow Israelite and the law of an Israelite father selling his daughter to another Israelite. These are terrible acts. What does this tell us about these former slaves? Shouldn't we have expected them to declare, "Free at last, free at last,

thank God we are free at last," and then speak about freedom and creating a society where all people are free? This example shows that it is hard, even impossible, for people to give up ideas they have had for years.

- We can see this problem of reluctance, inability to understand, or difficulty to change in the rabbis giving specific laws as in the Hebrew word *chok*. They defined *chok* as a law with no known reasonable basis. They gave the law of the red heifer as an example. Yet, Maimonides said that all the biblical laws make sense and explained the red heifer rule. The rabbis tried to make the general public comfortable with the regulations they called *chok* – which the general public could not understand – by saying that God has a good reason for the law that we do not know.

- Other examples. The biblical commentator Rashi states that Exodus 21 begins its list of laws with the Hebrew letter *vav*, which he translates as "and," and contends that the letter informs us that just as the Decalogue was given at Mount Sinai, so were the laws in Exodus 21 and the chapters that follow 21. The rabbis recognized that while what they were saying was not true, they felt people needed to think that these commands were so important that they were given to the people at Mount Sinai. It is like saying that God becomes angry when we misbehave, even though God has no emotions. We tell the general population that God becomes angry to frighten them into behaving.

- Plato called these false teachings "Noble Lies" and Maimonides "Essential Truths." The rabbis felt the general public needed to be told in various ways that the laws were given to us by God, who loves people and wants to help them.

- The rabbis changed all the laws listed above because these laws were appropriate for the generation of freed slaves who were unable to change, but were no longer applicable.

- While the Torah allows the continuation of misguided behaviors such as slavery given the mindset of the ancient people when these laws were promulgated, the rabbis understood that the Torah wanted better behavior. Therefore, the Torah allowed what the people considered proper, but hinted that the rules needed changing.

- The rabbis saw multiple hints of this. For example, if a Jewish slave wanted to remain in slavery beyond six years, the time limit in the Torah, this was permitted but frowned upon. The slave had to appear before a court that would try to persuade him to give up his idea. If he refused, his ear was pierced at the door post so that whenever he entered the house, he would be reminded by seeing the mark on the door that God wants people serving Him, not fellow humans. The rabbis found other anti-slavery rules later in the Torah.

- Examples of the Torah's attitude toward slavery is the law that no Israelite slave, even one sold by the court to repay what he stole when he lacks the money to do so, can serve for more than six years. Exodus 21:1–2 states he goes free without paying more, even if the court could not acquire the full restitution. In 21:26, if a master harms a male or female slave's eye or tooth, the slave is freed. This was because the Torah considered enslaved people human beings, not property.
- Besides the multiple hints in each Torah law suggesting the need to change it, the rabbis saw support for their ability to change Torah laws in verses such as Deuteronomy 17:8, "If there arise a matter too hard for you in judgment… then you should rise and go…and come to the priest, the Levites, and judge that will be in those days, inquire, and they will tell you the solution." Relying on rabbinical sources, Chief Rabbi Hertz states in his *Pentateuch and Haftorahs*, "Even if he be inferior to the judges who preceded him, you are duly bound to accept his decision." See also Deuteronomy 19:17.
- Deuteronomy 18:18 states, "I will raise for them a prophet like you from among their brothers. And I will put my words in his mouth, and he shall speak to them all that I command him."

OTHER LAWS IN EXODUS

- Among the "marital rights" for wives in 21:10 is the husband's obligation to have intercourse with her. This ensured that even in polygamous families, no wife would be neglected.
- In many societies, the altar was not only a place of worship, but also a place of asylum. This dual function is captured in the double meaning of "sanctuary." However, reflecting the Torah's desire to minimize the significance of the temple, 21:14 disallows the altar to give criminals refuge.

82 · HUMOROUS, SERIOUS, AND THOUGHTFUL IDEAS

- The rabbis interpreted that the selling by a father of a daughter involves a father giving his underage daughter in marriage to another man. However, it restricted the practice in many ways. He may not do so to a daughter who has begun a menstrual cycle. The money is, in essence, a dowry. If the purchaser decides not to take her as a wife after the purchase, she goes free when she has menstrual cycles, after six years with the man, or the jubilee year, whichever comes first. The purchaser may not give her to another man because she is not like cattle, nor return her to her father because he mistreated her by selling her. The purchaser may give her to his son as his wife, and she must be treated as any other wife.

- The rabbis in the Babylonian Talmud, *Bava Kama* 84 state that despite the Torah penalizing a man who strikes another, "an eye for an eye, tooth for tooth, hand for hand, foot for foot, burning for burning, wound for wound, stripe for stripe," the penalty is not inflicting the attacker with the same physical damage. Instead, different kinds of monetary payments are paid equitably, for the actual injury, the loss of time, the cost of the cure, the pain, and disfigurement. Some commentators insist that the money payments are implied in the Torah itself, or that these payments are part of the Oral Law that was given at Mount Sinai. Both views contend that God made it clear that only money payments were demanded. Others say it was the rabbis who changed the ancient harsh treatment.

- Hezekiah ben Manoah (1260–1310), in his biblical commentary, *Chizkuni*, notes that the prohibition against mistreating widows and orphans in Exodus 22:21–23 and the punishment for disobedience are written in the plural. In his explanation of the law, he shows the rabbinic teaching that people must love others as they love themselves and are punished for failure to do so. Even if people do not mistreat a widow or orphan, but remain silent when others do, they are punished.

- Why do those who insist that it was God, not the rabbis, who interpreted the words, and that what they called the "Oral Torah" was also given at Mount Sinai? They feel it essential to say that they need to believe in the divinity of the Oral Law for it to be mandatory.

UNKNOWN FACTS ABOUT THE BIBLE · 83

A FEW OTHER WAYS THE RABBIS INTERPRETED THE TORAH

- The biblical practice is to say something briefly the first time it is mentioned and elaborate upon it later. Examples include the Bible instructing Noah to take a pair of all land and air animals into his ark but later adding that certain animals were to be seven in number. Another oft-misunderstood example is that God created a man and woman in Genesis chapter one, while chapter two relates that the two were created separately. Many scholars and rabbis do not know the biblical practice, thus thinking that there are two versions of the story.

- In the Garden of Eden parable, Adam is told not to eat from a particular tree. Later, Eve states she was also told not to touch the tree. Again, many who do not know the biblical style later elaborated think that Eve received a different version of the divine command. The Torah tells us that the initial order included not touching the tree.

- Why was the second command not to touch the tree given? This, too, is part of the biblical practice. It is called placing a fence around the Torah so that Jews do not even come close to violating the law. The rabbis even extended this practice. An example is the rule of *muktzah*. On Shabbat, Jews are told, as the first humans in the parable, that they should not even touch an object forbidden to use on Shabbat. This "fence" protects the Jew from violating the Sabbath.

- In the parable, Eve misunderstood why she could not touch the tree. She thought she would be punished for touching the tree or eating its fruit. She did not know that the prohibition of not touching the tree was meant to help her not eat the fruit. When she touched the tree and was not punished, she thought she would not be penalized for also eating the fruit, and she ate it.

SOME VERSES HAVE AMBIGUOUS OR OBSCURE WORDS WITH VARIOUS
INTERPRETATIONS

- An example is the Hebrew slave in Exodus 21. Different rabbis give different interpretations. Another is Exodus 35:3, which states in Hebrew, *Lo teva'aru esh bechol moshvothechem beyom hashabat*. It means you must not make fire in all your homes on the day of Shabbat. But *teva'aru* could mean "burn," and the verse would be saying, no fire may burn in your homes on Shabbat. This is how the Sadducees understood the verse before 70 CE. They sat in the dark on Shabbat and in the cold during winter. But it could mean "light a fire." This would allow a fire if it were lit before the Sabbath. This is how the Pharisees at that time understood it. The rabbis accepted the Pharisaic interpretation and instituted the practice of lighting candles before Shabbat to remind Jews that Shabbat is a day of light and warmth.

Chapter Twenty-Nine
To Whom Do We Pray?

WHAT IS PRAYER?

Wikipedia defines prayer as follows, "Prayer is an invocation or act that seeks to activate a rapport with an object of worship through deliberate communication. In the narrow sense, the term refers to an act of supplication or intercession directed towards a deity or a deified ancestor." It is also defined as "to speak to a god either privately or in a religious ceremony to express love, thanks, or to ask for something like begging for help.

These are not Jewish concepts for rational-thinking Jews.

DOES THE TORAH TELL JEWS TO PRAY?

The rabbis disagree on whether the Torah mandates Jews to pray. Relying on *Midrash Sifrei*, Maimonides lists praying as the fifth and tenth positive commands of the 613 commandments.

The Torah speaks about "serving" God in several places, such as Exodus 23:25 and Deuteronomy 6:13. Despite no indication in the passage that "serve" means prayer, the midrash states this is what it means. Others, more realistically, say that "serve" means obeying the divine commands.

Maimonides also included among his list of the 613 commandments that Jews are obligated to recite the Shema twice daily because the rabbis in the Babylonian Talmud *Berachot* 21a saw this command in Deuteronomy 6:7.

86 · HUMOROUS, SERIOUS, AND THOUGHTFUL IDEAS

WHY DID MAIMONIDES SAY THESE THINGS WHEN THE TORAH DOES NOT EXPLICITLY REQUIRE THEM?

There are many indications in Maimonides' *Guide for the Perplexed* that Maimonides may not have believed that God needed or wanted prayers. These included his view of divine providence. He states in 3:17 and 3:54 that God is not involved in helping people. The divine gift of intelligence helps people. The greater the people's intelligence, the better chance they will have to help themselves.

As did Plato, who called it "Noble Lies," Maimonides believed in telling people what he called "Essential Truths." These untruths helped people feel good about themselves and aided in controlling their behavior. An example is "God becomes angry when people misbehave." This is not true. God has no emotion, as humans do. But the essential truth causes many to fear God's wrath and act appropriately.

WHAT LAWS DID MAIMONIDES INSERT IN HIS LIST OF 613 COMMANDMENTS?

Maimonides included laws that the rabbis felt were encompassed either explicitly, or implicitly in the Torah.

HOW MANY TIMES SHOULD A PERSON PRAY?

The Talmuds offer two purely speculative and sermonic reasons why Jews are told to pray three times each day.

1. Each service parallels the ancient sacrifices in the Jerusalem Temple until it was destroyed in 70 CE: the morning *Tamid* (a word meaning "perpetual"), the afternoon *Tamid*, and the overnight burning of this last offering.

2. According to Rabbi Jose bar Hanina, each of the three patriarchs originated one of the three prayers: Abraham in the morning, Isaac in the afternoon, and Jacob in the evening. He supported his view with biblical quotes, which he interpreted as indicating that the patriarchs were praying. However, the verses contain no hint that they were praying, nor indicate the time of their activity. Nor does it offer why the fourth Musaf service was created for Shabbat and holidays, or why an additional service was added for Yom Kippur.

Muslims must pray five times daily: *Fajr, Zuhr, Asr, Maghrib*, and *Isha. Salah* is prayed in the congregation every day at dawn, post noon, before evening, in the evening, and at night.

Roman Catholics are encouraged to pray seven times during the day and once at midnight. Each is three hours apart: *Lauds* is at 3 a.m., *Prime* is at 6 a.m., *Terce* is at 9 a.m., *Sext* is at noon, *None* is at 3 p.m., *Vespers* is at evening, *Compline* is before sleep, and *Matins* is at midnight.

While Muslims and Christians were break-offs from Judaism and adopted many ancient Jewish practices, and even the Catholic use of three and seven for their prayers – numbers often used in Judaism – neither the Muslims nor Catholics accepted the view of the Talmuds that three was the suitable number for daily prayers.

SOME MORE THOUGHTS ON PRAYER

Aside from the fact that many rabbis agree that prayer is not mandated in the Bible and believe that God does not personally help people, the following are additional ideas.

The Hebrew word for prayer rejects the idea that a person addresses God. The word *hitpaleil* means "judging oneself." It suggests that the individual uses the prayer words as a prompt for self-evaluation, a time to think about the past and future, and the resolve to take corrective actions to improve oneself and the rest of the world.

In contrast, as previously stated, the general population sees prayer as a time when people petition God for help.

Mystics spurn both views. They see prayer as a period of communion, a sense of joining with God when the individual finds contentment in being part of the whole.

Others feel obligated to pray because prayers fulfill what they consider a human requirement to praise God, and they mention many divine attributes, such as being merciful and compassionate.

Still others see prayer as a way of saying "thank you." These are but a few of the many other ideas about prayer.

THE PHILOSOPHICAL VIEW

Rational thinkers only accept the first view. God does not need prayer and does not hear them. The world functions according to the laws of nature and will not change no matter how passionately one requests that God alter nature. God is transcendent, and it is impossible to join with God. Extolling God for having specific attributes is insulting, for God cannot be understood, and whatever we say about God falls far short of what God is.

WHAT WERE THE PRAYERS IN THE TORAH?

"Prayers," as the word is used today, are unlike the prayers in the Hebrew Bible. The Hebrew Bible concept of prayers and the post-biblical versions are so distinct that one can safely say prayers did not exist in the Hebrew Bible. Why?

The Hebrew Bible pictures God as being anthropomorphic, a being one can talk to, just as God conversed with Adam and Eve in the Garden of Eden. Thus, when Moses requested God to do something, such as healing his sister Miriam, this was not what we understand as a prayer today. Moses requested God, with whom he had frequent conversations, and who he knew was very powerful, to heal his sick sister. Biblical people speak, cry, shout, and ask God, as one "person" talks to another, but they do not pray to God.

The Israelites offered sacrifices, but there is no evidence in any scriptural book that the sacrifices were accompanied by prayer. True, the Bible has psalms, but nothing in the Bible says they were used as prayers.

MOSHE GREENBERG

Moshe Greenberg, who died in May 2010, was a distinguished professor of the Bible. He called the biblical addresses of humans to God "prayers" in his *Biblical Prose Prayer*, but he recognized that they were conversations.[1]

Greenberg shows that these conversations are not formal statements, words, phrases, and sentences written by priests or poets, but regular human requests that focus on the needs of a specific person at a particular time. They are simple, to the point, and said by anyone, even non-priests, at any time and place. Thus, Moses' prayer on behalf of his sick sister, "God, please, heal her, please," was a simple request that Moses made to God, who was present, as soon as he heard of

---

1. The Taubman Lectures in Jewish Studies, Book 6, Reprint, 2008.

her illness. It was as mundane as a man needing money for a pay phone, turning to his friend, standing near him, and saying, "Frank, please, lend me a quarter, please."

Greenberg recognizes that some prayers start with "confessions," admissions by the petitioner that he did something wrong. The pray-er hopes that he can reestablish a good relationship and that God will grant his request. Greenberg stresses that this does not occur only in addressing God. People do this all the time when they request of others. "I'm sorry I did not call you last week, Frank, but could you lend me the quarter, please."

IN SUMMARY

It should be clear that the current understandings that prayers are a request, a self-analysis, a time of communion, or a need to praise God did not exist in the early biblical period. Personal prose encounters with God were simply conversations formed with the same informality as human conversations. Prayers, as we understand them today, developed later when people developed a feeling that God was not present but transcendental, loftier, and more inaccessible. This was when the people felt they needed to address such a deity with elevated formal language, words composed by experts, priests, and poets.

The best approach today is to treat prayer as a time for self-reflection, as indicated in the Hebrew word *hitpaleil*, which means "judging oneself."

WHAT IS THE PRAYER BOOK CALLED "SIDDUR"?

Jews use a prayer book called "siddur" for non-holiday praying and a "machzor" for holidays when special prayers are recited. Siddur means compilation. It signifies that the book has a collection of prayers. Machzor is based on a word meaning cycle. It refers to the prayers recited during the cycle of the many holidays.

Both books are compendiums. They are collections of different statements, ideas, requests, and copies of texts from the Bible, poems, songs, and other items. They were written and inserted into the prayer books by people with different ideas and motifs. Some ancient views are irrelevant today or do not fit our current ethical views. While we may disagree with some of them, they help us think and judge ourselves, as *hitpaleil* suggests.

90 · HUMOROUS, SERIOUS, AND THOUGHTFUL IDEAS

THE FOLLOWING ARE SOME EXAMPLES

There is a prayer inserted into the siddur by men who felt they were privileged to be able to keep all the 613 commands while women only needed to observe some of them. It is recited in each morning service. The prayer thanks God for not making them a woman. While the prayer is seen today by many as insulting, it should prompt the men who pray to think of their view of women in society, home, business, and synagogue, and work toward the goal still needed today of equality of all humans.

Another example is the Friday night service just before the traditional Maariv service, where a half dozen psalms are recited, and a song by the kabbalist Shlomo Alkabetz (c. 1500–1576) is sung. The mystics introduced this into the service. Many think the service's purpose is to welcome the Sabbath, but this is not true. The word Shabbat is in the song *Lecha Dodi*, but it does not refer to the weekly Sabbath. It refers to the messianic age. Without explaining the song here in any detail, I will summarize that the song seeks to join two elements of the *Sefirot,* which the mystics think bring about the messianic age once they are joined. Most non-mystics who do not know the origin and intent of the song, read into it the welcoming of the Sabbath, and think about how important the Sabbath is in their lives. Upon careful reading, it doesn't speak of the Shabbat. It is simply a poem describing a mystical idea that explains how a segment of Jewry differs from what they think.

Still another example is to turn to the siddur and follow an Ashkenazic[2] tradition in many families to sing Psalm 126, Shir Hamaalot, before Birkat Hamazon, the blessings following the eating of a full meal, on Shabbat and joyous occasions such as festivals, weddings, circumcisions, and Pidyon Haben.[3] Many scholars are convinced that this joyous psalm was composed when the Judeans returned to Judea after the Babylonian captivity in the sixth century BCE. The song speaks of the return: "When God returned the captives to Zion, it was like a dream."[4] Jews loved Shir Hamaalot so much that many religious Zionists, such

---

2. Ashkenazic Jews are from Germanic and other Western European Christian countries. Sephardic Jews originally came from Spain and thence from countries that were generally under Moslem control.

3. Some families add verses at the end from Psalms 145:21, 115:18, and 106:2.

4. Psalm 137 is sung instead of Psalm 126 on weekdays. It deals with the destruction of the Temple and the sad beginning of the exile in 586 BCE while Psalm 126 describes the

as Rabbi Tzvi Yehuda Kook, wanted to make it the national anthem of the State of Israel in 1948.

There is even a selection from the mystical book *Zohar*, a book that Jews with a rational life attitude reject, which is read and sung when the Torah is taken from the ark in synagogues on Shabbat. The melody is very catchy, and most congregants join in the singing. One can only hope that the day will come when the congregants realize that what they are singing about are ideas alien to their thinking, which come from the past that helped sustain Jewry. Hopefully, at that time, we will treat others as we want them to treat us and accept Jews and other people who have different opinions than our own.

THE MYSTICAL EXPLANATION FOR CHANTING AFTER EATING

The mystical book *Zohar*[5] explains the practice. It states that it is fitting to remember the Temple's destruction after eating because one who prays regarding the Temple is considered as if he built it.[6]

How do we interpret it as "is considered as if he built the Temple"? Mystics believe in sympathetic magic. When the *Zohar* states, "as if he built the Temple," it most likely means he is magically contributing to the building of the Temple.

Sir James George Frazer explained the phrase sympathetic magic in his justly famed book *The Golden Bough*, published in 1889. Frazer divided sympathetic magic into two kinds: relying on similarity, and relying on contact or contagion. He wrote that the two kinds prompted the idea that sympathetic magic works:

> The former principle may be called the Law of Similarity, the latter the Law of Contact or Contagion. From the first of these principles, namely the Law of Similarity, the magician infers that he can produce any effect he desires merely by imitating it. From the second, he infers that whatever he does to a material object will affect equally the person with whom the object was once in contact, whether it formed part of his body or not.

---

happy end. It was felt that singing Psalm 137 on joyous occasions was inappropriate as it begins, "By the rivers of Babylon, we sat and remembered Zion."

5. Parashat Terumah 157b.

6. The mystic Rabbi Isaiah Horowitz echoed the *Zohar's* teaching in his *Shney Luchot Habrit*, "Shaar Ha'otiyot, qof" 170. Other mystics did so as well.

92 · HUMOROUS, SERIOUS, AND THOUGHTFUL IDEAS

An example of sympathetic magic is the practice of American Indians dancing on the earth to cause rain to fall from heaven.

Although I haven't seen this idea expressed by anyone else, it seems to me that the two unique Sukkot practices – pouring water on the altar (which ceased with the destruction of the Temple) and banging *hoshanas* on the ground up and down (which is still performed) – were instituted as sympathetic magic. The practices were performed at the beginning of the Fall season when the rainy season began in Israel, and Jews wanted to ensure that the rain would be plentiful.

THE PASSOVER SEDER HAGGADAH SUPPORTS THE IDEA OF *HITPALEIL*
While people may find it hard at first to see prayer as a time for judging oneself, it is easy to see it in the Passover Seder's Haggadah. The word "seder" is the same as the prayer book's name, "siddur." Both words mean compilation. Both contain widely different ideas from various periods, focusing on multiple ideas. The word Haggadah means telling or narration. The book's function is to encourage family members and guests at the Seder to explore the meaning of the Exodus from Egypt, the ideas of slavery, freedom, education of children, miracles, and symbols. The rabbis said, "People who delve more into these subjects and discuss them are praised." The Seder aims to prompt participants to delve into matters that will improve them and society. This is the same method used by the siddur and machzor.

We also have rational and mystical ideas in the Seder and even another example of sympathetic magic when Jews recall the ancient exodus from Egypt and pray for the coming of the messianic age. It is the ceremony of opening the door for the prophet Elijah and its accompanying practice of placing a cup of wine for the prophet while reciting certain words. Tradition states that Elijah will reappear before the advent of the messianic age to announce it. To cause Elijah to come, the door is opened for him, and a cup of wine is poured for him. If we welcome Elijah on earth, it will, it is supposed, cause his appearance by sympathetic magic.

Similarly, the mystics developed the practice of turning around to the synagogue entrance at the end of their song *Lecha Dodi* when they sang about the coming of the Sabbath on Friday night. Why turn to welcome the Sabbath? As stated, mystics saw the weekly Sabbath as a symbol and foretaste of the messianic age. By turning to greet the "Sabbath," they were greeting the messianic age, and by sympathetic magic, they were helping it to come.

So, too, mystics thought that by singing about the Temple after eating, sympathetic magic would help in its rebuilding.

In short, using the siddur and machzor in the spirit of *hitpaleil*, which means "judging oneself," can improve individuals who are "praying." Individuals who do not seek outside help, but study the "prayers," to learn about the many different views of Judaism, improve their ideas based on these studies, thus increasing their knowledge, and using it to improve themselves and the world.

Chapter Thirty
What Do We Know about God?

Virtually all people are convinced that they know something about God. The truth is we know nothing. What we think we know is nothing more than wishful thinking. If so, what should we do?

In Exodus 33:18–23, Moses asked God to tell him what God is. Moses requests of God: "Please show me your glory," meaning, "Show me what you are." God replies that He will make the divine goodness pass before Moses, but He tells Moses that he cannot see His face. God instructs Moses to stand behind a rock. Then, after God passes, "You will see my back, but my face will not be seen."

Many ancient Jewish sages, including Maimonides, explained that God is telling Moses that because human intelligence is limited, humans cannot understand what God is. However, they can understand much about God by seeing and understanding what God has done, seeing God's "back." They know what God created. They learn about God by seeing and understanding what exists on earth and in heaven, thus the laws of nature.

After having this vision and knowing that Judaism requires two witnesses to attest to something, Moses tells us in Exodus 32:1 that he called as witnesses Heaven and Earth to reveal God. The prophet Isaiah did so also in 1:2.

Once we understand that the only way to know God is to see the world and learn how it functions, we realize that the fundamental teaching of the Torah, what God wants us to do, is to study the sciences. Many scholars have recognized this. In his 2011 book, *Maimonides the Rationalist*, Herbert A. Davidson states this and adds we should show our love of God by seeking scientific knowledge.

In his book *Apology*, the Greek philosopher Plato's account of Socrates' trial and death in 399 BCE, tells how Chaerophon, a friend of Socrates, traveled to the Oracle at Delphi and asked whether anyone was wiser than Socrates. The Oracle replied, "No man was wiser." Socrates explained he was the wisest because he knew he knew nothing with absolute certainty. Others thought they possessed knowledge they did not have. They were unjustifiably confident in their beliefs. Socrates was always skeptical.

Knowledge of the sciences helps us be all we can be and prompts us to help all that God created.

Many rabbis accept the idea that we cannot know anything about God, but say that there is no problem in thinking that God is all-powerful, knows everything, lives forever, and listens to our prayers and similar ideas, because even though we do not know this as a fact, it does us no harm to think it if it makes us feel good.

What is essential is not beliefs, but to act to improve ourselves and all God created and formed. Our first step to do so is to study sciences and see the "back" of God as did the two witnesses God set before us.

Chapter Thirty-One
Two Surprising Changes by Jews

The Judeans was the name Jews had in ancient times based on the fact that the people who lived at the time were in the area populated by the tribe of Judah. The name evolved into the word Jew when they considered the day and year began.

The year was 586 BCE. The Babylonians destroyed much of Judea and carried many inhabitants to Babylon. In Babylon, the Judeans encountered a culture far different than in Judea, unlike what the Torah required. Like their descendants, they were influenced by what they saw, foolishly thought the masses around them had good ideas, and adopted many of them. Their descendants did similar foolish acts, such as thinking beliefs were more important than acts.

The great rationalistic French Jewish thinker and Rashi's grandson Rashbam (Rabbi Samuel ben Meir) wrote a rational Bible commentary in which he paid attention to the wording of the biblical text and gave readers their actual meaning.

In his commentary on Genesis 1:5, he explains that the Bible clearly shows that the day began in the morning, not in the evening. The verse states that God did creative acts during the day, followed by evening and morning, the end of the day.

Jews initially followed the biblical timing. Most likely during the Babylonian exile after the First Temple was destroyed in 586 BCE, the Judeans accepted the Babylonian practice of starting the day at sunset. Scholars state that this was the timing used by the Babylonians during this period.

When many Judeans returned to Judea from the Babylonian exile and continued the revised practice, they did not change the temple service. When the Second Temple was constructed in 516 BCE, the day began in the morning as in the past. The first sacrifice was offered in the morning, and the sacrifices were left on the altar until the next day, which started in the morning.

The same phenomenon is seen in the Bible regarding the holiday of Passover. According to the Torah, it began on the morning of the fourteenth day of the first month and ended the next morning when the fifteenth day of the first month began. The holiday of The Feast of the Unleavened Bread began on the morning of the fifteenth of the first month. The two holidays did not overlap.

Rashbam's interpretation that the biblical day began in the morning explains why the Israelites could eat the Pascal lamb during the night of the fourteenth until the following morning. They could eat the offering until the next morning because the night following the day was part of it. It was still the fourteenth until daybreak.

Just as the Judeans accepted the Babylonian timing when they were exiled in Babylon when the day began, they also abandoned the biblical view in Exodus 12 that the year starts in the Spring, in the first month, the month of the Exodus from Egypt. Scholars recognize that when the Judeans were first exiled to Babylon, their neighbors felt the year began in the Fall. So they renamed the biblical holiday "The Day of the Trumpet," a holiday that the Torah created to recall God's seven-day creation by having Israelites blow the horn at the outset of the seventh month, just as seven was used for weeks, years (Shemittah), the seventh Shemittah is the Jubilee year, Passover and Sukkot last seven days, and many more uses of seven.

Not only did the ancient Judeans accept when the day begins (at sunset) and the timing of the new year, they also began to call the months by the names used by the Babylonians, even though one referred to an idol.

Moses repeatedly warned the Israelites, the name of the Jews during his lifetime, not to copy the ways of non-Israelites because he knew that it is human nature to copy the ways of our neighbors.

Should we try to stop imitating others? Should we stop saying beliefs are more important than acts? Perhaps we should emphasize instead the Jewish idea that acts are essential thus acting toward others as we want to be treated?

"The truth is the truth no matter what its source."

Sources

Abarbanel, Don Isaac. *Rosh Amanah*. Warsaw: 1884.

Albo, Joseph. *Sefer Ha-Ikkarim*, ed. Husik, J. Philadelphia: 1946.

Aristotle. *How to Innovate: An Ancient Guide to Creative Thinking (Ancient Wisdom for Modern readers)*. Trans. D'Angour, Armand. Princeton University Press, 2021.

Azariah de' Rossi. *The Light of the Eyes*. First print Mantuah, 1573. Translated by Joanna Weinberg. Yale University Press, 2001.

Babylonian Talmud tractates: *Bava Kama, Berachot, Chullin, Eruvin, Pesachim, Rosh Hashanah, Shabbat, Yevamot*.

ben HaKanah, Nehunya. *The Sefer Bahir: Book of Light*. CreateSpace Independent Publishing Platform, 2015.

ben Maimon, Moses (Maimonides / Rambam). *Guide for the Perplexed*. Translated by Michael Friedlander. Dover edition, New York: 1956.

ben Manoah, Hezekiah. *Chizkuni*.

Canetti, Elias. *The Memoirs of Elias Canetti: The Tongue Set Free, The Torch in My Ear, The Play of the Eyes*. Farrar, Straus and Giroux, 1999.

_____. *Crowds and Power*. Seabury Press, 1982.

Crescas, Hasdai ben Judah. *Sefer-Or Ha-Shem*. Maamar 3. Johanisburg: 1861.

Davidson, Herbert A. *Maimonides the Rationalist*. The Littman Library of Jewish Civilization, 2011.

Dawkins, Richard. *The God Delusion*. Mariner Books, 2008.

de León, Moses. *Zohar*.

Drazin, Nathan. *Legends Worth Living*. Ktav Publishing House, 1991.

Eylon, Dina Ripsman. *The Soul and Afterlife in Jewish Mysticism and Gnosticism*. Edwin Mellen Press, 2003.

Frazer, James George. *The Golden Bough*. Dover Publications, 2002.

Freundlich, Charles H. *Together Again*. Independently published, 2023.

Greenberg, Moshe. "Biblical Prose Prayer," *The Taubman Lectures in Jewish studies*, Book 6, Reprint, 2008.

Grossman, Jonathan. *Abraham: the Story of a Journey*. Maggid, 2023.

Hertz, Joseph Herman. *The Pentateuch and Haftorahs*. 5 vols. Oxford: Oxford University Press, 1930.

Horowitz, Isaiah. *Shney Luchot Habrit*. Lambda Publishers, Inc. 2000.

ibn Bilia, David ben Yom Tov. *Yesodot ha-Maskil*.

Jerusalem Talmud: *Berachot*.

Josephus, Flavius. *Wars of the Jews*.

Jospe, Raphael. *Torah and Sophia: The Life and Thought of Shem Tov Ibn Falaquera*. Cincinnati, Ohio: Hebrew Union College Press, 1988.

Kook, Abraham Isaac Hakohen. *Orot*. Translated by Bezalel Naor. Maggid 2023.

Lawee, Eric, "Maimonides in the Eastern Mediterranean: The Case of Rashi's Resisting Readers," *Maimonides After 800 Years: Essays on Maimonides and His Influence*. Edited by Jay M. Harris. Cambridge, MA: Harvard University Press, 2007.

Midrashim: *Sifrei*.

Mishnaot: *Berachot*.

Oppenheimer, Aharon. "Removing the Decalogue from the 'Shema' and Phylacteries: The Historical Implications." *The Decalogue in Jewish and Christian Tradition*. Edited by Henning Graf Reventlow and Yair Hoffman. New York: T&T Clark, 2011.

Plato. *Apology*, Bolchazy-Carducci Publishers, 1997.

Ruttenberg, Danya. *On Repentance and Repair: Making Amends in an Unapologetic World*. Beacon Press, 2022.

Scriptures, Megillot, and Apocryphal, and Pseudepigraphal sources (Pentateuch/ Prophets/Writings): Deuteronomy, Exodus, Genesis, Isaiah, Judges, I Kings, Leviticus, Luke, Matthew, Micah, New Testament, Numbers, Psalms.

Sefer Yetzirah.

Skinner, John. *A Critical and Exegetical Commentary on Genesis*. Charles Scribner's Sons, 1910.

Targumim: *Onkelos*.

Wiesel, Elie. *Rashi: A Portrait*. Nextbook, 2009.

Index

A

Aaron 42, 65, 76
Abarbanel, Don Isaac 37
Abraham 17–18, 21, 41, 55, 70, 72, 75, 86
Adam 9, 18, 28, 35, 38, 41, 83, 88
Albo, Joseph 37
Alkabetz, Shlomo 90
America 7
American Indians 92
anno mundi 17–19
Aramaic 76–77
Aristotle 25, 32, 38, 45
Asr 87

B

Babylon 91, 97–98
Babylonian Talmud
    Bava Kama 82
    Berachot 74, 76, 79, 85
    Chullin 72
    Eruvin 73
    Pesachim 74
    Rosh Hashanah 72
    Shabbat 38
    Yevamot 73
Bahir 31–32

bar Hanina, Rabbi Jose 86
Beethoven, Ludwig van 11
ben HaKanah, Nehunya 31
ben Manoah, Hezekiah 82
ben Nappaha, Rabbi Yochanan 42
Birkat Hamazon 90
British 7, 35

C

calendar 15, 17–19
Canada 7
Canetti, Elias xv, 51–52
chok 80
Christians 17, 79, 87
Compline 87
Cozbi 76
Crescas, Hasdai 37

D

Daily Telegraph 9
Danites 42
Davidson, Herbert A. 95
Dawkins, Richard 57
Decalogue 79–80
derashot 74
de' Rossi, Azariah 17

102 · HUMOROUS, SERIOUS, AND THOUGHTFUL IDEAS

Drazin, Rabbi Dr. Nathan 39, 45
Duran, Shimon ben Tzemach 37

E

Egypt 41, 49, 72–75, 92, 98
Elijah 92
English 7, 15, 77
Epicurus 56–57
Esau 41, 73
Europe 9, 51, 65
Eylon, Dr. Dina Ripsman 31–32

F

Fajr 87
Falaquera, Shem Tov ben Joseph 37
Frazer, James George 91
French 7, 97
Freud, Sigmund 52
Freundlich, Charles H. 47

G

Garden of Eden 35, 83, 88
Germanic 90
gilgul 31
Gomorrah 73
Gospels 5
Greenberg, Moshe 88–89

H

Haggadah 92
Herod 15
Hertz, Chief Rabbi Joseph Herman 81
Hesiod 63
Hitler, Adolf 9, 24–25
Horowitz, Rabbi Isaiah 91
hoshanas 92
Hoshea 75

I

ibn Bilia, David ben Yom Tov 37
ibn Ezra, Abraham 45, 71–72
India 7
Inquisition 7
Isaac 18, 21, 41, 70, 72, 86
Isha 87
Ishmael 41
Israel 7, 17, 47, 49, 73, 91–92
Israelites 17–18, 21–22, 41–42, 71–72,
    75–76, 88, 98

J

Jacob 41, 70, 73–75, 86
Janus 59
Jesus 15, 27
Jerusalem Talmud
    Berachot 79
Jethro 76
Jonathan 42
Jospe, Dr. Raphael 37

K

kavod 45–46
King David 3–5, 9
King Ferdinand II of Aragon 7
King Saul 18–19
Kook, Rabbi Tzvi Yehuda 91

L

Laban 70
Laish 42
Lauds 87
Lawee, Eric 74–75
Leah 41, 70
Lecha Dodi 90, 92
Luke 5

M

machzor 89, 92–93

Maghrib 87

Marie Antoinette 35

Mary 5, 15

Masorites 42

Matins 87

Matthew 5, 15

mezuzot 79

Midianite 76

Midrash
   Sifrei 70–72, 85
   Tanchuma 75

Miriam 42, 75, 88

Mishna 65

Moses 18, 41–42, 55, 65, 72, 75–76, 88, 95, 98

muktzah 83

Musaf 86

Muslims 17, 65, 87

N

Nachmanides (Moses ben Nachman) 32, 41, 70, 76

Noah 18, 73, 83

None 87

nun 42

O

Oppenheimer, Aharon 79

P

Palestine 7

Passover 39, 65, 92, 98

Pharaoh 72, 74–75

Pharisees 84

Philo 32

Pidyon Haben 90

Plato 32, 80, 86, 95

Prime 87

prophet 38, 81, 92, 95

Q

Queen Isabella I of Castile 7

R

ra 72

Rabbi Akiva 38, 42, 72

Rabbi Ishmael 71–72

Rashbam (Rabbi Samuel ben Meir) 70–71, 74, 97–98

Rashi (Rabbi Shlomo ben Yitzchak) 45, 69–77, 80, 97

Rebecca 41

Reish Lakish 42

Revere, Paul 35

Roman Catholicism 7

Ruttenberg, Danya 43

S

Saadiah Gaon 45–46, 71

sabriri 74

Sadducees 83

Salah 87

Samson 70

Sarah 41, 70

Scholem, Gershom 31

Seder 65, 92

Sefirot 90

Sephardic 90

Sext 87

Shakespeare 22

Shechinah 46

Shema 79, 85

Shemittah 98

siddur 89–90, 92–93

Skinner, John 45

Socrates 39, 95–96

104 · HUMOROUS, SERIOUS, AND THOUGHTFUL IDEAS

Sodom 73
Spanish (people) 7
Sukkot 92, 98

T

Talmuds 32, 72, 79, 86–87
Tamid 86
Targum
   Onkelos 76–77
Tell, William 35
Terce 87
Ternyik, Stephen I. 66
Tisha b'Av 65

V

Vespers 87
Vienna 51

W

Washington, George 35
Wiesel, Eli 69

Y

Yehoshua 75
Yom Kippur 39, 65, 67, 86

Z

zechut avot 72
Zimri 76
Zohar 91
Zuhr 87

Brigadier General Israel Drazin

Education: Dr. Drazin, born in 1935, received three rabbinical degrees in 1957, a BA in Theology in 1957, an MEd in Psychology in 1966, a JD in Law in 1974, an MA in Hebrew Literature in 1978, and a PhD with honors in Aramaic Literature in 1981. After that, he completed two years of post-graduate study in Philosophy and Mysticism. He graduated from the U.S. Army's Command and General Staff College and its War College for Generals in 1985.

Military: Brigadier General Drazin entered Army Active Duty at age twenty-one as the youngest US Chaplain ever to serve on active duty. He served on active duty from 1957 to 1960 in Louisiana and Germany. He then joined the active reserves and soldiered, in increasing grades, with half a dozen units. From 1978 until 1981, he lectured on legal subjects at the US Army Chaplains School. In March 1981, the Army requested that he take leave from civil service and return to active duty to handle special constitutional issues. He was responsible for preparing the defense in the trial challenging the constitutionality of the Army Chaplaincy; the military chaplaincies of all the uniformed services, active and reserve, and the Veteran's Administration were attacked utilizing a constitutional rationale and could have been disbanded. The Government won the action in 1984, and Drazin was awarded the prestigious Legion of Merit. Drazin returned to civilian life and the active reserves in 1984 as Assistant Chief of Chaplains, the highest reserve officer position available in the Army Chaplaincy, with the rank of Brigadier General. He was the first Jewish person to serve in this capacity in the US Army. During his military career, he revolutionized the role of military chaplains, making them officers responsible for the free exercise rights of all military personnel, requiring them to provide for the needs of people of all faiths and atheists. General Drazin completed this four-year tour of duty with honors in March 1988, culminating in thirty-one years of military duty.

Attorney: Israel Drazin graduated from law school in 1974 and immediately began a private practice. He handled virtually all suits, including domestic, criminal, bankruptcy, accident, and contract cases. He joined with his son in 1993 and formed offices in Columbia and Dundalk, Maryland. Dr. Drazin stopped actively practicing law in 1997 after twenty-three years.

Civil Service: Israel Drazin joined the U.S. Civil Service in 1962 and remained a civil service employee, with occasional military duty until retirement in 1990. At retirement, he accumulated thirty-one years of creditable service. During his U.S. Civil Service career, he held many positions, including being an Equal Opportunity Consultant in the 1960s (advising insurance company top executives regarding civil rights and equal employment) and the head of Medicare's Civil Litigation Staff (supervising a team of lawyers who handled suits filed by and against the government's Medicare program). He also served as the director for Maryland's Federal Agencies' relationship with the United Fund.

Rabbi: Dr. Drazin was ordained as a rabbi in 1957 at Ner Israel Rabbinical College in Baltimore, Maryland, and subsequently received *semichot* from two other rabbis. He entered Army active duty in 1957. He left active duty in 1960 and officiated as a weekend rabbi at several synagogues, including the first rabbi in Columbia, Maryland. He continued the uninterrupted weekend rabbinical practice until 1974 and then officiated as a rabbi intermittently until 1987. His rabbinical career totaled thirty years.

Philanthropy: Dr. Drazin served as the Executive Director of the Jim Joseph Foundation, a charitable foundation that gives money to support Jewish education, for just over four years, from September 2000 to November 2004.

Author: Israel Drazin is the author of 56 books, more than 500 popular and scholarly articles, and over 10,500 book and movie reviews. His books include one about the case he handled for the US Army and a dozen scholarly books on the Aramaic translation of the Bible, Targum Onkelos. His website is www. booksnthoughts.com.

Memberships and Awards: Brigadier General Drazin is admitted to practice law in Maryland, the Federal Court, and before the U.S. Supreme Court. He is a member of several attorney Bar Associations and the Rabbinical Council of America. He was honored with military awards, the RCA 1985 Joseph Hoenig Memorial Award, and the JWB 1986 Distinguished Service Award. Mayor Kurt Schmoke of Baltimore, Maryland, named February 8, 1988, "Israel Drazin Day." A leading Baltimore Synagogue named him "Man of the Year" in 1990. He is included in the recent editions of *Who's Who in World Jewry*, *Who's Who in American Law*, *Who's* Who in Biblical Studies and Archaeology, and other *Who's Who* volumes.